They Call Me Jabe

They Call Me Jabe

A Hillbilly Tale of Life, Death, and Grace

JABE LARGEN

RESOURCE *Publications* · Eugene, Oregon

THEY CALL ME JABE
A Hillbilly Tale of Life, Death, and Grace

Copyright © 2025 Jabe Largen. All rights reserved. Except for brief quotations in critical publications or reviews, no part of this book may be reproduced in any manner without prior written permission from the publisher. Write: Permissions, Wipf and Stock Publishers, 199 W. 8th Ave., Suite 3, Eugene, OR 97401.

Resource Publications
An Imprint of Wipf and Stock Publishers
199 W. 8th Ave., Suite 3
Eugene, OR 97401

www.wipfandstock.com

PAPERBACK ISBN: 979-8-3852-5280-0
HARDCOVER ISBN: 979-8-3852-5281-7
EBOOK ISBN: 979-8-3852-5282-4

VERSION NUMBER 092525

Scripture quotations are from: New Revised Standard Version Bible, copyright © 1989 National Council of the Churches of Christ in the United States of America. Used by permission. All rights reserved worldwide.

For my children, my family, and those I remember,
who visit me in my dreams.

Contents

Preface | ix
Acknowledgments | xiii

    February 2007 | 1
1 Origin | 3
2 Grounded | 7
3 Paw-Paw | 11
4 Road Brothers | 14
5 Shift | 19
6 Dabbling | 21
7 Crumbling | 27
8 Hard | 32
9 Paw-Paw Part Two | 36
10 Almost | 39
11 Potential | 42
12 OC's | 48
13 Regional | 51
14 Love | 57
15 Indictments | 60
16 Graduation | 65
17 Miriam | 69
18 Roadrunners | 73
19 Gabriella | 80
20 Methamphetamine | 83

21 Undone | 87
22 Reuniting's | 94
23 Awakening | 99
24 Damascus | 103

    February 13th, 2007 Revisited | 106

25 Bethany | 107
26 Maw-Maw Fisher and Others | 111
27 Wall | 115
28 Diapers | 118
29 Where? What? | 123
30 Faison | 127
31 She | 130
32 Ashes | 134
33 Darkness | 138
34 Bethany Revisited | 142
35 Elegy | 146
36 Kairos | 151

Preface

It wasn't until my second year of pursuing a master's degree that I realized that it is pronounced "*preh-fiss*" as opposed to "*pre-face*." When some friends later in life made fun of another friend for not knowing the proper pronunciation, I joined in the heckling as opposed to admitting that it wasn't that long prior that I did not know what to call it either. Whatever you call it, never did I think I would be writing one. The only reason a preface would be needed is if a book had been written. Why would I ever write a book? Over half of my life, I haven't enjoyed reading books, much less writing them.

I was twenty-six before I read my first book as an adult. I grew impatient waiting for the 5th Harry Potter movie to be released, so I bought a book, and then another, and then another. Prior to the Potter books, the last time I read one cover to cover was fourteen years earlier, while in the 7th grade; it might have been fifty pages.

Yet here we are, in the preface of a memoir, written by me despite all my years of non-book-ness. My motivation for writing this unlikely and unexpected memoir came from a few places. For one, I wanted the story of my people to be told and remembered. When I say my people, I am using the term as an expression to name the people who I have walked through life with, in the places I have called home. They are my people, just as I am their people. They are and were, good people. The stories of my people are stories worth sharing because they are told about people, who like their places, have tremendous sacred worth. As for the people this rings true, be they living or dead.

Speaking of the dead, at this juncture in life there is a desire within my spirit to tell some true tales, and to allow the living of my people who have left this life to continue through the memories and imaginations of others. Death is a constant theme in my story, sometimes appearing as a friend

Preface

bringing relief, most times as an enemy entering uninvited. Death in many ways serves as one string that holds much of the narrative together. My hope is that the other string woven throughout this story, the one known as "life," ultimately proves to be the string above all strings, holding all things, including death, in their place.

At times, in talking about matters of living and dying, it may seem as if I am being overly critical of my original homeplace in Appalachia. It has never been my intention in life to present that place as ugly or unfit for quality living. It is not ugly, and it can be a quality place for living for some. I love that place and sometimes find myself with a strange longing for it. I do hope that in this elegy, the Appalachian home, and the people I know there, can receive my words not as disrespect, but as an honest retrospective of one life lived in a place that is loved, during a challenging time not just for me, but for many in our region.

It is also the case that Pulaski, Virginia has experienced some revitalization in recent years (in certain places), and that should be celebrated. I also hope those who read this story who are not from that area, can view its people with the honor and respect they are worthy of as good, human, people from a good, and beautiful, sacred place.

As is the case with the medium of memoir, what is found in these pages is my perspective of the truth of my experience. There are others from that place, and other places, who have their own perspectives, truths, and experiences from the times I am recollecting. I firmly believe most of us who were in Pulaski the time that I am writing about, in most of what follows, can agree that the main themes with which I deal are presented truly and would be agreed upon from almost all perspectives.

The second place that I called home is mentioned some within these pages, but far less than the original place. Despite living there for ten years, most of my story as I am telling it, is set in my place of origin due to the depths with which that home shaped me and led me to the life I lead today. There is an abiding love for that second home and its people in the flat lands of eastern North Carolina. Although not talked about a lot in these chapters, I hope the love that exists shines through, if not these pages, then my life, like the beautifully surreal sunsets that can often be viewed in that patch of creation.

My current home in one of the primary golfing destinations in the United States is only mentioned a little, again, not due to a lack of love, but for the same reasons noted above. Make no mistake, all three places have plenty of stories worth being told. Each place also consists of many people I have journeyed or continue to journey with, who are worth mentioning, but go unmentioned. No slights intended. One volume of a cohesive and readable narrative requires the exemption of some notable nouns.

In addition to telling the stories of my people, I came to concede that my story could serve a purpose in offering people hope. I believe there to be billions of far more remarkable and resilient people in the world than I. There are also lots of stories I would deem to be far more compelling. With that said, at the urging and support of some of those closest to me, I took up this project because of the potential that exists in offering hope in a world that can often feel hopeless, especially to those experiencing trials similar to mine. Were it not for the hoped-for hope, nothing would be bound and published.

Prior to beginning the chapter portions of the book, it is important to note that my writing style is one that will make use of various expressions that may not be familiar to some readers. Also, my vernacular is very much that of someone raised in Appalachia with some eastern North Carolinian mixed in. Hopefully, it doesn't take too long to get used to vernacular and style. My native vernacular is far less prevalent in my formal writing now as opposed to when I first started writing formally nearly twenty years ago. After all, eventually the cows must come home, or, if you believe in karma, the chickens will come to roost.

You will see as you read, this story involves a lot of death, trauma, and tragedy. My third reason for wanting to take this on was selfish; I needed to get a lot of what is suppressed within me out. The experience of getting the words correlated with the memories was not easy. Reliving all the death, trauma, and tragedy took a toll on me in more ways than one. It took a lot of grace for me to have breath in my lungs long enough to make it to this point in life where I have this unlikely and unexpected opportunity to tell this story. My selfish hope was realized in that now that this storytelling process is complete, I have found that there was sufficient grace to allow for much of the closure my spirit and mind longed to receive. In so many areas and ways in which I was previously unsettled, I now find that glorious and unearned, peace which surpasses understanding.

Finally, in a word of disclosure, this story is not only filled with death, trauma, and tragedy, but it is also filled with drugs, alcohol, violence, mental health matters and thoughts on societal problems. If a sentimental encounter or a feel-good story is what you are anticipating, I encourage a

Preface

shift in expectations before reading. The themes listed in the first sentence of this paragraph are far more prevalent than any sort of sentimentality.

I probed the hidden depths of my soul and wrung its pitiful secrets from it . . .

—Augustine, *Confessions*

Acknowledgments

I AM NOT HERE, nor am I who I am, without the love and support of my family. Now, and especially when I got clean over twenty years ago. Likewise, I am not alive were it not for the love and support of those in the recovery community, namely in the New River Valley area. Because of anonymity, I will not name you, but you all know you who are. Because of you, my gratitude speaks.

Many thanks are due to Kyle Burrows, Katie Hoerster, Jim Gulledge and Paul Cocco. Each provided tremendous feedback that helped frame the narrative of my life experience, while forcing me to confront and confess some truths that I was avoiding having to confess. I am deeply appreciative for all the readers, not only by helping shape the content of my narrative into something readable, but for also providing all the comma criticism, and other editorial type functions. I have learned that if you can get three out of five people who write or have extensive grammatical experience to agree on where a comma should go, you have achieved something special.

I am beyond grateful daily for the good folks at Pinehurst United Methodist Church. The PUMC community is unique and such a gift. I am humbled to be in their midst. To the leaders who made possible my time away in the Summer of 2025 to do the heavy lifting needed for this to be published, I can't thank you enough. All in all, for PUMC and my gratitude, there are far too many reasons to list.

To the communities of Pulaski, Faison, and Moore County: Thanks for allowing me to call your home, my home, and for being such good places and good people.

To those who are often named in this work, and to their families, I love you. You and your loved ones are a part of me. Thanks for not writing me off all the times that you could have, and probably, rightfully should have.

Acknowledgments

At this juncture, it is appropriate to give thanks to the person who was most present during most the times revisited through the telling of this story, Amber Largen, my wife. Much of the darkness written about is a shared darkness. It has taken a tremendous amount of courage on Amber's part to allow me the opportunity to tell the story from my perspective. I owe her much gratitude, not just for sharing the journey, but for having the strength to support me in this phase of journey sharing.

Finally, thank you to all the institutions, teachers, and mentors that have taught me. Hopefully as you read, at times you will notice, despite my grades, I was actually paying attention.

February 2007

*18 months without the use of narcotics,
the longest stretch of my life since the age of thirteen*

My cousin Dina lived with her parents on the other side of Maw-Maw and Paw-Paw Largen's for all of her and most of my childhood. She was always on the short side of things height-wise. She had her father's dark hair, and for most of childhood wore thick rimmed glasses. Dina's mother was basically adopted by Paw-Paw's parents when she was young, back in the mid-to-late 20th century. Although not blood, she and Dina and husband Manny were always 100% family.

I fondly recall playing on Dina's little, aluminum-framed swing set as a child; she had the only one on the hill. I also remember all the reprimands shouted out from across the yard by my Paw-Paw, telling me I was too big to be on it. The fact that as I swung, the aluminum structure would rock off and then back on the ground should have been my clue. Although she was a handful of years younger than me, swing set or not, I enjoyed being around Dina in our childhood. I think anyone who spent time around her enjoyed her company. It would be hard not to.

When Dina was twenty-two, in February of 2007, she had a gastric surgery. The idea behind the surgery was to allow her to lose weight and therefore become healthier. Those surgeries were commonplace in those days, and so long as the patient did their part, they often proved to be a great success. I wish that were the case for Dina; she never got the chance. There was a complication from the surgery that went undetected until she got home and became extremely sick. She was rushed back to the hospital where she soon died. Her parents were devastated as were all the rest of us who knew and loved them and her. She truly was one of the sweetest souls I have ever known, and when she died in 2007, I could not help but think, it should have been me who was dealt such fate and not her. It *should* have been me.

I was the kid who grew up on the hill with the drug problem and the history of mischief and deviancy. If life and its decisions and actions were all subject to a court of law, I would be found guilty more times than not. Dina was the kid who grew up on the hill who sought only good and did only good; truly innocent. We were opposites, and if fairness from the human perspective is the paradigm by which all things in life are judged and then ultimately unfold, then yes, it would be me dealt an early demise. It wasn't. Fairness seldom seems to play a part in matters of living and dying. For whatever reason, it just doesn't work that way.

February 13th, the day before Valentine's Day, was the night of Dina's funeral service. The family gathered into the chapel at Stevens Funeral Home, and as was the custom, received visitors through a receiving line prior to the service. I remember hugging Priscilla, her mother, who remained seated on the tiny chapel's front pew and saying, "I don't know what to say, but I love you." She responded, "You know what it is like to hurt. You know how some of this feels." Maybe there was some truth to what she said. I was still overwhelmed with the thought, "That is supposed to be you. You should be the dead one. You deserve it."

Deserve is a lot like *fairness*. As I have grown in my knowledge of words and how those words correlate with a life of faith, I have come to believe that the word "deserve" is one that has little or no theological significance on how things unfold in triumphs or tragedies, or in general. In an existence that is made possible by way of a gift of a loving Creator, what could ever be *deserved*?

With that said, when Dina died, I had little capacity for theological pondering. I had plenty of capacity at that stage in life for feeling, and I felt as if she did not deserve her fate, and if anyone near to her life did, it was me.

1

Origin

IN THE APPALACHIAN FOOTHILLS there is a place that to many is just a name on an interstate exit sign as they make their way to Roanoke or Bristol, Winchester or Syracuse, and/or all sorts of places in between. Pulaski. Virginia to be exact. The namesake of a Polish Count who was known as a brave and noble leader of calvaries in the U.S. during the American Revolution. He was so brave and noble in fact, many states in the southeastern U.S. adopted his surname as their town name. Around Savannah was as far as the Count and his heroism could make it; a round of grapeshot got him. His body lay there to this day. You can't see his actual body lying there in Savannah, although they do have a statue. Pulaski has one too.

Take the aforementioned exit off of I-81 into the Virginia version of the Count's legacy and you will see a town that is not at all dissimilar from other Appalachian towns all along the mountain line. Gas stations that sell a lot of lottery tickets and cigarettes, a few fast-food places, some more gas stations (which is ironic given the number of people you see walking), a Methadone Clinic, a shady motel, a once-great furniture factory that is actually comprised of more than ten factories on one footprint. Find your way to Route 11 in town and you will find a gas station turned fruit stand, another shady, dilapidated motel, a buy-here pay-here car dealership, a closed gas station, a closed flower shop, low income apartments, the remnants of the foundation of the bar that burned down thirty-five years ago when I was a boy, and yet another gas station (still a lot of people walking).

Turn left in front of that gas station, known by many names depending on how long you've been around Pulaski (it's still Pack-n-Sack or F&R

to me) and you are on Alum Spring Road. A road that matters to me. A road that formed me. A road that leads to home.

About a half mile down the narrow, curvy, tree-lined, two-laned Alum Spring Road, just before you get to the red barn (all that was in that barn in my younger years was a little straw and some hidden Playboy's) you will find the narrow Snider Lane on your left. Michael, Keith, and Winky grew up on the Lane. Veteran's Hill breaks off of the Lane as well, this gradually inclining, twisting and turning road is lined with small homes, and was a part of my friend group's wandering territory for many years. Like all these roads, I know Veteran's Hill like the back of my hand.

Stay on Alum Spring past Snider Lane or see Snider Lane to its completion back onto Alum Spring, and you will pass what is now the old Jordan's Chapel building. A white wooden church by a slow-moving creek (I shot a basement window out with a BB gun while on top of Winky's roof once. Winky said I was going to hell for it). This is a church that I would one day (unpredictably) speak in from behind a little wooden pulpit.

Not far past Jordan's Chapel are Friend's Store (not a store, but they did have a wine closet), and the picturesque rock quarry behind it (Keith would climb it). Above the quarry is a field my friends and I used to run around in (Keith would pick up hardened cow patties and throw them at us).

From the Friend's place you are a stone's throw from the turn onto Largen Hill Court, which sits across from another hill where Adam lived. From atop either hill, and during most of the way along Alum Spring's curves, you can catch a glimpse of mountains in the distance, rolling hills, livestock, wooded-lands, occasionally a few white-tail deer, all things of beauty that make Pulaski County an aesthetic gem from a natural world perspective.

Surrounded by the unique beauty of Pulaski County, if you do turn right off Alum Spring Rd. onto Largen Hill Ct., and make it to the top of the hill, then turn left, you can spot the third house on the left, a faded brown double-wide sitting on two acres. The place that was set-up in 1985 for Sammy, Sherry, and their only child; they call me Jabe.

To this day, lots of folks like to ask if Jabe is short for something. The answer is no; it's just Jabe. The name of my great-grandfather, the father of my paternal grandmother, they called him Jabe Keith. His wish was for someone in the family to inherit the name before he died; I was the last chance. It's a good name, especially if you are doing good things. It's a bad name only when you do bad things. It's much harder to get recognized for good and much easier to avoid consequences for bad if your name is Bob or Dan. Better or worse, there's always only one Jabe.

The last name is Largen (pronounced: Large-in), just like the name of the hill that the double-wide sits on. The Largen Hill home was the second home I remember having as a boy. Prior to landing there on a plot of land given by my Paw-Paw and Maw-Maw Largen, we lived further down Alum Spring Road, May Street, first house on the left. It was a charming, smallish, brick, ranch style home with a carport almost as wide as the house.

One of the cool things about the house on May St. and later the home we would make on Largen Hill Court (also known in those days, pre-911 addresses, as mail route 172) was the proximity to Loving Field. Something to know about me, to understand the excitement of this proximity: I love sports like squirrels love nuts. Loving Field housed eight fields to be exact, some for softball, some for baseball, some for both, and soccer too. All eight were carved from a former airfield, each one separated from others by four-foot-tall, chain link fence.

When we were in the May St. house around the time I was four years old, I remember my dad's friend, out of the blue, showing up at the house fresh from Loving Field to receive medical treatment. He had slid into a base and received one of those nasty skin injuries known in bat and ball sports as a "strawberry." I remember him hovering his right butt cheek over our bathroom sink, whilst wearing a jock strap, wincing and screaming in pain as my parents laughed while pouring rubbing alcohol over his wound. The sight of the wound enamored me. I was equally caught up in what may have caused it and what else happened. What type of heroic play did he make? Was he safe? Did they win? When is the next game?

It was a couple of years later when that same friend showed up on Largen Hill bearing gifts. He worked at a sporting goods store and had brought me some items, knowing I was sports obsessed. This wasn't cheap stuff. There was a set of shoulder pads, a football helmet, and batting gloves. He was obviously drunk. After he left, mom and dad gave each other a look, she mouthed, "I wonder if he stole them." This was my first glimpse behind the curtain that adults often put up to shield their progeny from the harshness of adulthood and things like alcohol and substance abuse. I remember the feeling in the pit of my stomach when I watched her mouth those words, and realizing the curtain had been torn and I now realized that my adult heroes were fallible and capable of things like theft (drunkenness was ok still).

Not long after that night, I rode along as my dad went to visit his friend at St. Albans, a large, three-story brick psychiatric sanitorium (now a haunted house attraction) where he was being treated for addiction. That was the first time one of my heroes fell from grace. It would not be the last. Of course, I would have many falls of my own; I hope I was no one's hero.

As I grew in age in that Largen Hill house and then in other houses, Loving Field strawberries were quickly replaced with new wounds, not in the name of sport, although shooting was involved. As is the case with any self-destruction, one will quickly find they no longer give a hoot about things that once mattered, nor about the people and places that formed them. And they sure as hell don't care where or what home is. One of the most cunning aspects of addiction is the way in which it creates voids in one's inner-being where there were none previously, while simultaneously widening the voids that already exist.

Here I modify and reinterpret a parable of sorts that I once heard to make the void point clearer: imagine you are in a frigid house with no fire. You decide to tear away some of the boards on the side of the house to create a fire. As the fire gets bigger, the draftier the house becomes. The process continues until there are no walls remaining, and because of this lack, the fire naturally sizzles out. That is addiction, and the voids it creates and widens. As the addiction progresses, the amount used needs to increase accordingly. Thus, causing bigger and more voids, until all that is left is no structure and only a little sizzle.

Eventually, the voids become so daunting, the only thing that remains is death or indictment. I have dodged one outcome. I certainly felt like I qualified for them both. The funny thing about grace is, sometimes it prevents certain outcomes and in other instances it doesn't. When I have inquired of God as to the reason why grace is funny like that, all I have received back in response is, "No comment."

2

Grounded

FOR THE MAJORITY OF my adolescence on Largen Hill Court, when you first turned on it from Alum Spring Road, you would first pass by the Burton's shack on the left. The Burton kids were always dirty, perhaps a byproduct of the reality that in terms of plumbing they had none. Only things they had in that category were an outhouse and one of those hand pump wells like you see in Western's or on *The Andy Griffith Show*. Their clothes were always tattered, their hair always unkempt. The youngest one's feet were always bare.

Just past the Burton's place on the other side of the road was the school bus driver and his wife. They kept a good garden in growing months that was just as green as the shutters, shingles, and deck on their otherwise white house. Mary and her family were the next house, just at the crest of the hill. Sweet Mary rode our school bus, her dad served in Desert Storm. For years, a yellow ribbon hung on their only tree in the yard, a walnut.

Once you hit the crest of the hill, on the right was Aunt Alma and Uncle Neal (Little Neal died from an injury sustained while in the Navy). Their house was one of only a few to have a fence in the yard. Across from them, Aunt Ruby and Uncle Junior, and then later Manny and Priscilla and my cousin Dina. Beside them, Maw-Maw and Paw-Paw Largen. Across from their place was an older woman and then the Giles family (I am told my Paw-Paw ran in and saved the older woman when her kitchen once caught fire). Beside the house with the new kitchen was a little five-room white house that belonged to my dad's first cousin and best friend Michael. We called him Duck. I was told he ran one like, but faster. Beside Duck was his mom and dad, Aunt Betty and Uncle Elwood. Uncle Elwood and

I would keep a big garden beside of Alma and Neal's for a couple of years until one morning the ambulance came and picked his lifeless body up. Paw-Paw and I would tend the garden after that.

Just below Betty and Elwood's and across the yard from Maw-Maw and Paw-Paw was our double-wide with a fair amount of wooded land behind it. Beside of us was the New Life Tabernacle Church (they were a fiery bunch, brimstone aplenty), and rounding out the top of the hill, Jimbo Linkous and family, who built on land beside his parents, one of whom was Jim Linkous, the well-known seller of live fishing bait.

Back in those days, the hill always felt safe. It had a tinge of what might be called an Americana feel to it. A typical day in nice weather you would find Alma and Neil on the porch, Dina on the swing set, Maw-Maw in the flower beds, Paw-Paw outside of one of his building restoring some antique or junk item, me in the yard or on the sidewalk pretending I was in the NFL or MLB if I wasn't next door in the church parking lot pretending I was in the NBA.

Uncle Elwood would be tinkering in the yard or with his truck or picking up and putting decaying apples in a five-gallon bucket for he and I to take to feed an old nanny goat. Aunt Betty would be tinkering too, add an occasional car passing by to get some nightcrawlers or minnows (pronounced *minners*), wash, rinse repeat until winter; do it again next year.

Blood relation or not, neighbors helped neighbors. There was a shared life on the hillside. If one had apples, all had apples, even the goats. If one had green beans, all had green beans. If a neighbor fell, five would be there in an instant to help them up. Thus was the rhythm of life for most of my childhood. On the hard clay and rocky ground of that hillside, I was blessed to be raised.

Not only did I have the family on the hill, but as a young boy, I also had the Loving Field family to help raise and form me. There were a lot of them, including the previously mentioned friend with the strawberry. In warmer months, two nights during the week I would be at Loving Field under the lights watching my dad and his friends and teammates win a lot. The sounds are etched into my memory. The *"thupp-tink"* sound that a softball bat makes when good contact is made. The calls from the outfield and the bench, "hum-now, hum-now," "hey now," "here we go now," "pick me up," "put him down," and my favorite: all hands in and then slowly rising out of the huddle with the chant *"heyyyyyyyyyyyyyy."*

The smells are hard to forget too. The smell of the dirt. Loving Field dirt smelled different. I can best describe it as an earthy chalk smell. There was also the smell of fresh cut bluegrass. The smell of leather when everyone was in on the bench. Concession stand hot dogs, another distinct smell. Yet the most prominent smell of them all, cigarette smoke. As I recall, almost all of them smoked, our team and the others. In a strange sporting rhythm, when it came time to return to the bench to get ready to hit, they each lit a cigarette. Prior to returning to the field, they each lit another. In modern times, in Minor League and Major League ballparks around the country there are countless in-between inning promotions and activities such as dizzy bat races and mascot's wielding tee-shirt cannons. Our fields had Marlboro's and Winston's.

The postgame festivities in the mostly dim parking lot were where the most fun was to be found. There were coolers full of beer, jokes being told, more beer, more cigarettes (of both the left- and right-hand variety), comradery, brotherhood, shenanigans, steam relief, celebration, coping, team building, family time, bullshitting. What happened in the parking lot could be known by many names. All I know is that I loved it. These were my heroes.

Some weekends, the family known as the Lee Riders (sponsored by the company most of them worked for at the time) would hit the road and head to an out-of-town tournament multiple hours away. One weekend in the mid-80's, the Riders were in Winchester, VA and I was allowed to pack my ball gear into an old bat bag and tag along. From the comforts of a motel room one evening, I heard a ruckus on the balcony (motels have entry doors outside, hotels are more internally focused; like a mystic or a monk).

Like any curious kid who wants to belong, I jumped up to see what the fuss was about. There, this man who I admired and respected (the eldest of the denim brand heroes) was yelling at his son, who was about 18-years-of-age at the time. The younger man, also a member of the team had gotten tore up from the floor up, pee-pee pants, fall down drunk. It was not a rare occurrence for most of the team to get in such a state, or close to it, but what made this instance so offendable to the father was the fact that his boy had done this at the young age of 18 and in the presence of people who could actually hold their beer, and out of town on a trip at this fine motel. The team rallied around the older man and offered words of warning to the boy, many doing so with the smell of Coors on their breath, and/or with a can in hand. It was on that balcony that I first heard the ancient words of some unknown prophet, "Do as I say, not as I do."

A year or so later, we were at my dad's boss's house for a party. Of course, the whole team was there, including the pee-pee pants boy. There he was, throwing down Coors with the rest of the gang. No one seemed to care. It was that same night I also witnessed, along with a rather large group of kids about my age, a co-worker of dads falling into a bush prior to launching vomit on the side of a hill behind the house. We kids gathered around and laughed, much the same way this guy and others had gathered around the young man and scoffed not so long before. There he was now, wearing a short-sleeved button up shirt that was halfway unbuttoned, his chest bore the green of Kentucky bluegrass stain, his chin bore a slight remnant of his stomach's one-time contents. His eyes were rolled partially back into his head. After a moment, much to our pleasure, he began to laugh with us.

Despite the disturbing sights and sounds of watching this man's body fight back against his drunkenness, you could never convince me at that age that there was any more admirable a group anywhere. These guys were the epitome of cool. They played ball, and they won, they partied in the parking lot, they partied at each other's house, then they repeated the cycle again. My deepest desire at that age was to be just like them. Although a fan of major leaguers, given the choice, I would have chosen the two nights a week at Loving Field and the occasional tournament away. And I would have chosen it time and time again, and gone on playing and partying the rest of my life. A fair amount of my life, especially in the early to middle years was centered around the pursuit of that desired reality, or one similar. To no avail, of course. Apparently, living that sort of idealistic life requires an intricate balance that I am not capable of maintaining. Whenever I have tried to achieve that life, I find it has been far too easy for me to fall off balance and end up in a bush.

I had my first taste of beer at age eight. We were at another party with the Lee Rider gang. This first beer, among others, were stolen that night by one of the older kids present from a communal cooler. Coors, the banquet beer, via Golden, Colorado. After chugging away in the camper that we kids were allowed to hang out in during the party, I threw up. That night, unlike others to follow, I managed to dodge the bush.

3

Paw-Paw

His name was James Alford Largen. He was a Korean War veteran who they say was a mighty fine pool player. In the service he had the opportunity to play the great Minnesota Fats. Minnesota challenged him and swore to use a broom stick instead of a pool cue to make it fair. Knowing who this billiard legend was, and being no dummy, James Alford Largen stepped down from his eight-ball king of the company throne and allowed some other GI the opportunity to be embarrassed. And he was. My Paw-Paw said the other kid never got to hit the first shot, Minnesota ran them all in, with the stick end of the broom of course.

Paw-Paw Largen was a man of slight build; slight but solid. For the time I knew him, and for most of the photos I have seen, he wore a weathered, wrinkled face and bushy eyebrows. Just above the eyebrows, in almost the center of his forehead, he wore two large cyst-like growths that he never complained about or even mentioned. His hands were always calloused. He installed carpet for a living, prior to retiring and getting involved in the antique business. My Maw-Maw would have told you that it was mostly junk, but there were some quality pieces every now and then, like a Victrola, a China cabinet, metal toys, a playing piano, or an old armoire or trunk.

The restoration of the junk, or antiques, was a full-time job for the man, and he seemed to love every bit of it. Day in and day out, he would be found outside of one of his buildings down on one knee in his Dickie's brand pants, button up shirt mostly buttoned, some hat that had been given to him by some salesman on his head, with a lit Doral hanging out of his mouth, sanding and/or staining this or that, getting it ready to sell at an upcoming Flea Market. The constant aroma around his buildings as he worked was that of paint thinner and dust.

The intentionality with which Paw-Paw worked was admirable. With each swipe of sandpaper, with each brush stroke applying lacquer, with each installation of new hardware, he thoroughly enjoyed watching old things that some may label as junk come back to life. That is a trait that he and I share, although in different ways. Knowing him, I would say that he probably predicted his only grandson would turn out like the renewed junk one day, given the right craftsman and handiwork.

He was not only my Paw-Paw and my neighbor, but in those early years of life on the hill, he was my best friend. It was Paw-Paw who took me the most places as a young boy. With both of my parents working, and with our shared affection of one another, and with our proximity to one another, it worked out that way. He and I would go to historic Calfee Park to watch the Pulaski Braves of the Appalachian League play baseball. He would always make sure to buy me some hard vanilla ice cream served up in one or another Major League's team's mini-helmet (he made sure that I had them all). It was Paw-Paw who took me to Delton to fish by the guard rail for red-eyes or white bass when they used to run up the river. If it wasn't Delton, it was to the Lighthouse or Rock House to catch a mess of bluegill that we would take back to the hill where Maw-Maw dropped them in hot grease boiling in a cast iron skillet, which then lead to many minutes of picking bones out of our teeth. Seemingly every evening there was somewhere to go and something fun to do thanks to rough and gruff, Doral-smoking Paw-Paw.

It was Paw-Paw who drove me down to the bottom of the hill each morning to catch the school bus. In the winter months, the heat that rolled out of the vent above the floorboard of his brown Dodge Ram set my legs on fire while allowing the rest of me to remain frozen. There at the bottom of the hill on those frosty mornings he would ridicule Boonie Breedlove who was on the other side of the road trying to keep my friend Adam warm while he waited on the bus as well. "Look at that crazy Boonie Breedlove. Sitting over there with his windshield not even half defrosted." I would've looked, but many of those mornings I couldn't see through the frost on my side of the truck windshield.

Paw-Paw Largen was also the one who never missed a baseball game in which Jabe played. As I stood in the dugout and peered out past the outfield fence, without fail, his brown truck could be spotted, strategically positioned to catch all the action, smoke rolling out the window. When I got home, I could count on some thought-provoking commentary from the old man regarding my performance from his perspective from the other side of the fence. One night I hit a homerun to end a game in Draper. When I got home, I ran over to see Paw-Paw. "Paw-Paw, did you see that game winning homerun I hit?" My number one fan said, "Yeah, I saw it. That was a single with three throwing errors. And the score was 15–0. You didn't win the game, you ended it by the slaughter rule." If I scored twenty points in a basketball game, he would ask why I didn't score twenty-five. I didn't mind the commentary. To be sure it did not hurt my confidence. To this day, I cherish the memories of his playful banter.

It was Paw-Paw and Maw-Maw who greeted me as I walked through the yard after my first day of Kindergarten, and I remember their raucous laughing as I lamented at how long and hard of a day that it had been. They continued to greet me for the years that my Maw-Maw Fisher didn't greet me at the Fisher homeplace on the dead-end side of Newbern Rd in town.

On more than one occasion, I got off the bus at the bottom of Largen Hill and motored my way up to find Paw-Paw laying out in a random part of the yard, smack dab in the middle of the grass, hat not on his head, but near his side. Thinking he was dead each time, I would rush to his side and shake him, only to be greeted by a grumpy old man who fussed at me for waking him from his nap. Turns out, bluegrass, despite its sharp edges and bumpy blades can make a rather comfy bed. That is, if you don't mind sharing a sleeping space with worms, ants, grasshoppers and fleas. I guess one day, it won't matter if we mind sharing an earthy bed. We will rest with them through no choice of our own.

4

Road Brothers

I NEVER REALLY LIKED school. I understand how strange a claim that is for someone who spent twenty-four years as a child and then an adult learner to make; it is true, nonetheless. In those early years, it was my friends who made school bearable. I did not have many friends early on in life, to be honest. Other than the imaginary ones that I played sports with daily, there was Adam from the hill across the road, and my dad's best friend's son named Matt, and that was it. It would not be until the 4th grade that I would make another friend, a friend who, in the years to come would become my best friend.

Winky was his name. I knew him to be a bit rough. He wasn't all that big of a fella, not scrawny, but wiry. He had dark black hair and a slightly dark complexion, earning him a couple of other nicknames later in school: "Chavez" and "Navajo." Although named after a cool character from the *Young Guns* movies, he didn't love his unsolicited new names. The questioning of one's true ethnic identity was common in that place in those days. Sometimes it was meant for jest, most times the aim was harm.

Speaking of harm, Winky was not scared to get in a fight with kids that I would want no part of in any tussle. He took up boxing like his daddy, also known as Winky. They were known individually as Big Wink and Little Wink when we were coming up. Both were tough.

The two Winks' and the rest of the family lived in a blue house at one end of Snider Lane, behind the little white church by the creek on Alum Spring Road. There were several homemade and occupied chicken coups behind the house, and commonly a majestic German shepherd dog in the front yard named Maverick who terrified me, but never did me any harm.

After Maverick's days came to an end, he would be succeeded by a clumsy hound pup named Copper, who once took a chunk out of the side of my face. I, unwisely, went to pet the pup while he was chowing on his chow, his instinct kicked in, and my cheek bled out.

Long before Copper, my face took another blow. Around the 4th grade, Winky and Adam had become good friends and began riding together on the school bus in the same seat. I was not offended by this in any way, but apparently Winky thought I may have been. One day as I sat in the seat in front of he and Adam, Winky said something to me that rubbed me the wrong way. I said something in return, witty, no doubt, and then Winky stood up. While my head was still turned to him, he reckoned that I could be good boxing practice, so he punched me right dead in the nose. That was my first punch in the nose. It would not be the last. Not even from Winky.

I got off the bus and sprinted up the hill, eyes still watering from his precise blow to my nose. Getting tagged in the nose always leads to watery eyes, even if the tagging itself does not make you cry. I eventually shook off the pain and the shock, and about thirty minutes later, another shock: Adam and Winky making their way up the hill to play basketball in the church parking lot next door. Adam was always playing peacemaker for our group, even if at times he first played instigator. Adam was tough too. Like Winky, he was wiry, but strong, very strong. He was fast as lightening, even while wearing the tight blue jeans of our youth. He almost always wore a hat over his dark hair. Later in life he often wore a goatee. Long before the days of facial hair, the three of us played basketball in the church lot, the very same day I got punched in the nose, Winky and I became the best of friends.

Keith and Michael would be a big part of this friend group as well. Michael was the smallest of us all. In the earlier years of our friendship, he was slightly round, with curly blondish hair touching the top of his back. Later he would grow taller, and the roundness would vanish. He almost always had his lip poked out with a big pinch of dip.

Keith had a stout build and mostly dark hair. He went back and forth from a shaved head to a haircut similar to that of Adam or Michael, not quite a mullet, but close. Like most of us, Keith was light complected and tended to walk with a sort of half skip when we were younger. It is hard to explain, it was an interesting quirk. It was almost as if he were riding an imaginary horse, and every now and then, the horse would giddy up. Oddly and hilariously, almost always, Keith would make a clicking sound prior to his skip walk.

Michael, Keith, Adam, Winky, and I all lived within a couple of miles of one another, on the previously mentioned hills and lanes off of Alum Spring Rd. As we got a little older, our families had less issue with allowing us to roam the roads and hills and hollows (pronounced *hollers*) around our neck of the woods. The five of us would wander and wonder our way around, discovering this and that along the way, talking about Lynyrd Skynyrd, girls, and other matters of importance, day in and day out for years. Once we discovered a way through the woods to Leisure Lanes, the Pulaski bowling alley. Over the years, many days and nights were spent at the bowling alley, shooting pool and misbehaving.

Speaking of misbehaving, a lot of what we discovered on our wanderings was mischief, what I have come to more commonly call shenanigans. All five of us were individually wired for shenanigans naturally. When the five of us got together, we were straight up trouble. We were smoking cigarettes and dipping long-cut Skoal and chewing Redman or Levi Garrett tobacco on our little trips up and down the roads and through the hills, as early as the 6th grade. I would regularly swipe a pack of Doral's out of Paw-Paw's truck when he wasn't looking, Keith would convince his mom to buy him the cans of dip, or we would get an older friend to buy some for us. We never went without tobacco products. The game of not getting caught by the parents who would object to our usage (like mine) was a fun game to play. Not getting caught by the ladies at the little white church's youth group was as equally fun a game. "Quit running around here like a bunch a rednecks!" is a refrain we would often hear.

Most of our youth group activity involved dipping snuff and trying to flip over rocks to catch crawdads in the creek that ran by the church. To catch a crawdad, you must slowly turn the rock over, trying your best not to startle the creature. Once the little bit of underwater dust settles, you reach and grab as quick as you can. I was the worst of the crawdad catchers. The reasons for my crawdad catching inadequacies are probably many. I will say that I did not like making two of the shell-backed captives fight to the death as much as some of the others enjoyed it.

Michael would also catch little corn snakes and let them slither around in his mouth if he first chose not to kill them by treating them like a tomb raider cracking a whip. When once asked by a church lady as to what his daddy would think about him playing with and killing snakes,

Michael, with a little brown tobacco spit dribbling down his chin said, "He'd be proud."

Keith got kicked out of youth group a lot, even though his aunt was one of the leaders. Usually, his ousting would come because of the words that would come out of his mouth. We all said those bad words, but Keith could care less about where he was when they flew out of his, and church was no exception. What little church ladies refer to as "reverence," Keith had none. The same lack existed when it came to most forms of necessary restraint.

Keith was tough. Arguably the toughest of the group, even if Adam whipped him often. The toughest one may not win every fight, but it is how bad of a beating you can sustain that determines overall toughness.

Keith stayed in different classes in school than the rest of us, mostly because of his behavior, and perhaps, although unconfirmed by me, because he had some learning disability. He spent a fair amount of time in the juvenile detention center in Christiansburg and a harsher one, which was more of a maximum-security type place for juveniles called Beaumont during the time of our middle school and high school years.

As alluded, there were often fights amongst us and often, when he was around, Keith was involved. There came a point in time, I don't remember when, that he stopped fighting back. Even though he was the toughest of the group and could fight for minutes on end, eventually he assumed the role of punching bag. I suspect the consequences he had been facing due to his behavior and some of the counseling/coaching he had received in the places of his consequences had encouraged him to take on more a passive role. I am ashamed of all the times we beat on him for virtually no reason while he curled up in a ball. Once, I soaked his light-weight, fatigue style camouflage jacket that he was using as a winter coat in water and put it in a freezer and then kicked him out of my place because he had done some small thing to tick me off. What a jerk thing to do. On another occasion, I took a baseball bat to the rims of his new bike. I thought he had stolen some money from me. I later discovered he hadn't. Like I said, jerk moves. The thought of my doing these things, brings me great, yet deserved, guilt and shame. Unfortunately, some things can no longer be made right.

We eventually learned there was a much healthier way for us to be violent with one another: shooting at each other with bb guns. That was short-lived. Like some of our bodies, and one of our lips, my mom's grey Cutlass once took a bb, while I was in the passenger seat. Mom heard the sound but had no idea what it was. I looked under the bridge where we caught crawdads, there stood Keith, bb rifle still raised. My other brothers were jumping up and down behind him gleefully. Part of me wanted to fight all of them in that moment. At the same time, the other part of me wanted to jump up and down with them.

The next iteration of fully consented violence occurred when we started boxing in Michael's basement. The problem was we only had one set of boxing gloves. Therefore, somebody had to deal with the disadvantage of the left-handed glove. I remember being the left-glove wearing fool one day, as Michael (the smallest of us all, and I the biggest) got inside of my reach and repeatedly hit me with uppercuts on the jaw and jabs in the nose. Nose punishment, what fun! It would not be long before all of us stopped hitting each other in the nose and started punishing ourselves by putting things up our nose instead, by way of a cut off straw, or a rolled-up dollar bill.

5

Shift

ONE DAY WHEN I was in the 8th grade, very early in the school year, aged thirteen, my mom walked out of the front door of the brown cedar sided house we called home and started making her way up the sidewalk toward her car (we became a two-car family in 1988 a few years after we moved into the house on the hill). As she made her way up the inclined, rough-poured concrete sidewalk, I inquired where she has going, and she said, "the store." I, being a slight momma's boy, exclaimed that I would like to join her. She told me I wouldn't like this trip, as she was simply going to the drugstore to obtain some feminine products. I insisted that I would not mind tagging along. She very reluctantly agreed for me to get in the car. As we reached the bottom of the hill, prior to the left turn onto Alum Spring, she informed me that we were not going to the drugstore to buy feminine products. She was going to look at an apartment, and since I was so adamant on tagging along, I would be looking at this apartment with her.

My mind raced, "Why are we going to look at an apartment?" I didn't have to be too smart of a guy to start figuring it out. She was leaving my dad. To be honest, I didn't see it coming. They spent all their time in separate rooms when in the house together, dad in the spare bedroom turned den, mom in the living room. We didn't do anything together anymore. Dad had retired from softball and worked a fair number of hours. We did bowl together a bit. A lot of time was spent by dad at his parents' house next door, which I think was a contributing factor to the things getting to the point that they did. Nevertheless, I didn't expect it.

Mom and I rolled up to this picturesque gate that opened into a long driveway and a beautiful lot. A large brick home, about two miles as the crow flies from Largen Hill, sat on an exceptionally large lot for a house in town (we lived outside of town limits. This is an important distinction. We were not town people, we lived in the county/country). We were greeted by the homeowners who led us down around the left side of the home to where the basement apartment opened past a sliding glass door. The ceilings were seven-foot from the ground, made of the white tile common in schools, hospitals and church fellowship halls. They were low to the ground, and they encased the large fluorescent lights also common in schools, hospitals, and church fellowship halls. Several painted concrete poles were scattered throughout the basement apartment, providing stability to the structure above. It had a nice kitchenette with a little bar, two bedrooms, and an appropriately sized bathroom. This was the apartment that one of my mom's best friends had moved into when she had left her husband some years prior. It was just familiar enough.

We left the apartment and headed back home. My mom is an emotional person and although determined and ready to make the move, her heart hurt. I know it mostly hurt for me. Later in life, I would discover that her heart also her for herself, and my quite a bit for my dad as well. With that said, she knew this move in life would not be easy, but it was what had to be done at the time it had to be done. The following Wednesday we sat down as a family and had the tough talk about the separation. Tears were shed, hearts were broken, life would change.

To this day I have no ill will toward either of my parents for the way our family split. What matters most, is they both did the best they could with their only son, together and separate, and I love and thank them for it. With all of that said, be there correlation or not, it would be a short-time after the split of my folks that I would begin the process of becoming undone, from more perspective than just one.

6

Dabbling

Head on out of the basement apartment's one way in and one way out sliding glass door, run down the grassy hill to the bottom of the lot and through the parking lot of F&R Market, and I would find my feet on Alum Spring Rd. Still only being a short walk away from my friends and the places we roamed made things bearable, as did the fact that I was now dating a girl who lived very close to the new apartment. She and I were becoming quite connected with one another in the 8th grade, so I didn't mind the move at all. I was the starting quarterback and safety on the 8th grade football team, I had a girlfriend that I was head over heels for, I was in all honors classes, well-liked, and well-supported even though I had just become a child of divorce. In addition to those things, I was also on the brink of my own destruction, yet at the age of thirteen, I didn't realize it. Much like the side of the interstate as you enter Pulaski, there were signs.

When time came for summer football two-a-day practices to begin prior to my freshman year of high school, out of insecurity and lust, I decided not to play football and to instead spend my summer with my girlfriend. A tremendous amount of time was spent at the local tennis courts where she had found love for the game and, truth be told, I liked it too. Often, Winky tagged along, which made it even more enjoyable. One of my favorite games to play was the two of them against me. I probably didn't win much, since they both were good, but it was a way for me to flex my athletic ability and stroke my ego. I've always been super competitive; most of the time (until my forties) to a fault.

That summer, my ego and competitive nature both took substantial blows when I entered a regional tennis tournament sponsored by everyone's favorite fast-food chain. My first match was against a kid a foot and a half shorter than me from Blacksburg named Inmar. Not only was Inmar considerably smaller than me, but he was also a couple of years younger than I. Inmar whooped me. Badly, he whooped me. That summer on the hard, steamy, green concrete courts outside of the county high school, I learned I would not be a tennis star.

Looking back, I needed the discipline that the football two-a-days would have brought into my life way more than I needed time with a girl or a tennis racket. My dad, and his parents, were certainly the main source of discipline in addition to my mom throughout my earliest formative years. After the divorce, my time spent on Largen Hill Court was minimal. The arrangement was, I was to show up on Wednesdays and Sundays to spend time with dad and the family there. It quickly turned into Sundays only. The more I started partying my freshman and sophomore years, the less time there was to commit to visiting my dad and other kin on the hill. When they did happen, the hill visits consisted of my sleeping in the floor of the living room, most times because I was behind on such rest due to lots of partying.

My Maw-Maw Fisher, who was also like a best friend, loved me too much to keep hitting me with the switch (tiny wooden stick) after I got to a certain age. Paw-Paw Fisher was always working 10-hour shifts in the furniture factory, so discipline from him was not on the table. Now, with the new arrangement off the hill, there was little time spent around any of the disciplinarians outside of my mom, and in what I believe to have been compensation for our leaving dad, she stopped disciplining me for the most part as well. Some tough coaching would have done me well. I am convinced that football in 9th grade would have set my life on a totally different trajectory. As much as it would have helped me, I'm grateful I didn't do it. Gratitude for the moments of the now make such regrets null and void (most days).

Eventually, as is the case with many young romances, my girlfriend and I broke up. It was her choice, not mine. Well, technically, it can be said that it was in part brought on by my calling upon another girl over the telephone and her finding out. I have found that when you are in the wrong in a situation, memories become fuzzier.

Shortly after the no-no phone calls went down, my girlfriend had been romantically linked to a much older boy. I think they got to fancy one another in a community church youth choir. Teenage hormones fly around those type things as densely as musical notes. Soon, all hell broke loose, and things fell apart. When I say hell broke loose, what happened was, she would not answer the phone (in the days of landlines only), which led my suspicions to take the mile or so walk to her house where I found his car in the driveway and she on the kitchen counter with him kissing on her. Which then led to the things falling apart piece which began with me kicking a late 80's model Mustang. Don't worry car enthusiasts, it was the cheaper LX model and not a GT. My anger had standards. They would get married after college and have a beautiful daughter.

With that relationship officially fallen apart, it was time for me to fall apart. I would not fall apart alone. Now, my main support system would be my mischievous group of friends, our little band of brothers. It was around this time that we all branded ourselves with hot ends of lighters or heated up clothes hanger wire in a sign of solidarity and brotherhood. Branded, and being good by-products of our environment, we began smoking pot and/or drinking alcohol on a daily basis. By the time I reached the age of fifteen, not a day went by that I was not using some sort of mind- and mood-altering chemical with my friends.

One of my first loves were benzodiazepines, such as Xanax, Valium, and Klonopin. These sorts of pills were easy to procure in all my years of using in Pulaski. Everyone knew at least a few people who had prescriptions that were willing to let a few pills go for a buck a piece. The great thing about this type of medication, other than its affordability, is that I could eat a handful of tiny pills and feel absolutely nothing and remember absolutely nothing. I was a kid who was now struggling with severe acne and a boat load of other issues with identity, belonging, and family. Feeling and remembering nothing was quite welcoming.

One day in the 9th grade, which I do not recall with any sort of vividness, I swallowed a few Xanax and passed out in Geography class. It was a test day. The following day when I returned, my test was returned to me. I made a zero. The test paper had a large dried up drool spot to accompany a squiggly line of ink that went from the top to the bottom of the page. Nothing legible. Come to find out, a longtime friend woke me up at the end of class and she had encouraged me to just guess answers prior to handing in my test. The squiggly line was my attempt at making twenty letters to serve as responses to twenty multiple choice questions.

On another occasion soon thereafter, I ate a similar number of Xanax and got in such bad shape at school that the school nurse became involved.

She called my mother who rushed me down to the end of the hill that the school sat upon to see a doctor. The diagnosis was simple, I was tore up. High. Gassed. On one. Nothing unusual about that. Getting tore up was the thing to do. She could have saved that copay, had they listened to me, or more accurately, had they been able to understand what I was trying to say through my incoherent, slurred speech.

Staying as high as possible for as long as possible was the thing to do those days, not just for us, but for most of the community around the roads that we ran. It was common in those days for my friends and I to spend our days and nights drunken and stoned or pilled up in various shacks occupied by some older person or another. We knew aplenty. One of my favorites was the house of a female friend's mother. What made it so enjoyable is that the mother could sing, but she was only willing to once she reached a certain level of drunkenness. When she did sing, she sounded just like Patsy Cline. Her belligerent boyfriend said he took her to Nashville so she could try and make it, but as he would say often, "She was just too damn ugly."

Most of our up and down the road days and nights began at the bus stop by the white church. There we would wait for our bus and smoke as much pot as possible in the allotted time before Cecil the bus driver showed up. If pills were available, we would eat or snort those at the bus stop as well. There were a couple of instances at the bus stop and another place before going to school, where we would take some psychedelics in the form of paper acid (LSD) or mushrooms. Never was that a good idea.

One Friday night on Robinson Tract Rd., just beyond Loving Field, Winky and I had consumed a fair amount of psychedelics. At that time there was paper acid floating around that we called "Hearts and Crosses." The paper acid comes as a full 5x7 sheet containing one hundred individual "hits" (doses) that gets stripped into ten hits per strip. With the "Hearts and Crosses," every other hit there was an alternating pattern of hearts and crosses on the back side of the sheet and therefore the strips as well. One hit heart, next hit cross, so on and so forth.

I don't remember if I ate a heart or a cross that night, perhaps both. Whatever it was, the strength of this batch of acid led to the night which began on Robinson Tract to be strange and surreal. When we arrived, acid already disintegrated on our tongue, we discovered that the house we were at was well stocked with *Natural Ice*. A little-known fact to most, a psychedelic trip can turn even wilder with a case or two of strong malt beer.

That entire night I would run (or stagger) in and out of that house on Robinson Tract to see some of the most spectacular sights I have ever beheld in the sky. I would drag others out onto the tiny wooden porch, who much to my chagrin, couldn't see the same things in the cosmos I was beholding. My favorite sight on that trip were long, tubular clouds, rotating like tornados yet parallel to the ground as opposed to toward the ground. It was a vivid and quick funneling of these clouds in a patchwork fashion that had me completely awestruck. The funnels were moving and connected and as real to me as the nose on my face.

If the church ever embraces "micro-dosing" we may come to call such visions as glimpses of the Kingdom's glory. However, on that evening, as the night wore on, the tripping wore off and the interweaving spinning clouds disappeared. There was no glory, only a strange feeling of drunkenness caused by lots of beer and a waning amount of a psychedelic trip from some once strong LSD.

Winky and I were left in the early morning hours with a long trek back to the basement apartment. Staggering from all the beer, but still functioning well enough to go someplace, we made the journey homeward. At one juncture, we stopped along the way to throw rocks through this guy named Chip's picture window; can't say why. He was one of the people on Veteran's Hill we would go and get messed up with on our daily journeys up and down the road. It was just drunken meanness I suppose. After the rock tossing, we stopped to talk to Travis, who was our age, and like us, on a good one that night. Travis had already dropped out of school and had begun shooting up dope; some new drug, Oxy something or other they called it. I say we stopped to talk to Travis, but his speech was not exactly understandable at that point in the early morning. Who knows what the two of us sounded like?

Just before reaching the path to the basement apartment, the sky lit up again, this time with amazing blue lights. Attributing it to the trip lingering, we continued to walk on down Alum Spring Rd. The cop behind us insisted we stop, now with not only lights, but sirens. We were asked about the window at Chip's house on Veteran's Hill, to which we replied, "It wasn't us, but you know Travis, we saw Travis up there, you should probably talk to him." The cop gave us a ride to my mom's apartment and dropped us off, no more questions asked. We shot pool until the sun came up.

There were many nights akin to that night on Robinson Tract for the whole of our crowd. My friends and I were teenagers in high school in the pursuit of a good time. Pills, pot, psychedelics, pilsners, by any means necessary. Bus stop, bus seat, Veteran's Hill, Robinson Tract, on the road, or in a shack. What began as a search for a buzz because I witnessed my adult heroes catching one as a kid had quickly escalated into something that was rapidly becoming out of my control. I'm not sure how it happened, I just know that it happened fast. Whenever, wherever, my people and I were always in search of a good time, until the good times faded and all that was left was the hard and sometimes dangerous work of the search.

7

Crumbling

BACK IN THE GLORIOUS days (late 70's and 80's) that my dad and his friends played softball, Pulaski County, VA was a somewhat thriving place in terms of its economy. There were lots of industries employing a lot of individuals, not just from Pulaski, but from many other places around the region. Some folks would come all the way from West Virginia, an hour or more away, to work in our county. We had furniture factories, a truck manufacturing plant, and more textile businesses than you could shake a stick at. Slowly, things began to decline. Much of the blame for the decline of the area should rightly be placed on the genesis of the global economy and the mass exodus of textile/furniture manufacturing jobs as a result of NAFTA. What was once a thriving rural community quickly unraveled into a narcotic stricken place of increased poverty and sickness that some referred to as *Little Chicago* or *Pu-ville* or *Pill-aski* or *Pill-ville*.

As I entered high school, our homeplace was experiencing a sharp decline in its economics, its quality of life, and in its outlook on the future. The area, and many of her people, would become depressed. More and more, as factories closed up shop, dope usage became increasingly prominent and deadly. This new reality was the case for people of all ages, races, and socioeconomic statuses. The change was rapid, the decline was steep. Things and places that once shone with a Norman Rockwell-esq character, now began to bear the dullness of plight. Businesses that were once staples in the community began to close shop. Many of the people who were once jovial and full of life in softball field parking lots and places the like, quickly became hollowed out versions of their former selves.

It was during this timeframe that some of my friends and I became not just casual users, but heavy users, of dope and beer. In this coming-of-age season, surrounded by community decline, I remember Keith bragging about smoking crack and being appalled he would do such. All I could remember were the Nancy Reagan commercials on television telling the youth of America that crack was whack. The one commercial that really stood out was the one with the egg; people from the 80's will remember "this is your brain on drugs." I also remember the Just Say No and D.A.R.E. campaigns in elementary school where for one of them, a deputy brought into the classroom all the real-life samples of all the bad drugs that we should not never do. If we promised not to touch the stuff there before us for the rest of our life, we got a sticker. Despite Nancy's best efforts, it wasn't long after hearing about Keith's crack experience that I would have my first encounter as well.

One day, Winky headed home from the bus stop and walked up onto his front porch which overlooks the church by the creek. There, he found several large bags of pot and several large bags of a hard white substance. He had at this time a young hound dog named Copper. At some point during the day in his roaming (everyone's dog roamed in those days) Copper had sniffed out a large supply of dope from a nearby dealer's house on a washed out, unpaved road on a hillside off Snider Lane called Barbara Lane. A man by the name of Clem rented out one-bedroom shacks that were often occupied by the type of folks like the person who had the misfortune of having Copper on their property that day.

Copper had to have worked hard to bring all that dope back. It had to take multiple trips from the lanky, black and tan hound. No doubt, his mouth was numb. And there it was, what we would later learn was thousands of dollars' worth of crack and pot, on the front porch, by the front door of Winky's blue house, a gift from the dope gods and a clumsy, hardworking, and thoughtful hound pup.

To verify what we were dealing with was indeed crack rock, we enlisted the help of my friend Matt's older brother Jon. Matt's brother was well regarded by most dopeheads as the coolest guy in the school. He was a senior when we were freshmen. He was another hero of mine. Always had been, even before dope. He knew all about drugs, in their many forms and fashions. He was the epitome of a drug dealing youth. Where my dad and the guys from the rowdy softball days had previously been what I aspired to be, now it was people like Matt's brother Jon; still rowdy, but in a different kind of way; pockets full of dope and money, and a great sound system in a cool looking little car.

Jon showed up in his little red two-seater hatchback with the bass booming. He asked to see the puppy-acquired rock. He broke off a fair-sized chunk of it, places it in a pipe and lights it up. His eyes got big, and his cheeks puffed out like a blowfish. He exhaled the toxic, yet sweet smelling fumes, with a deep sigh accompanied by the words, "Yeah, it's crack." Winky had several ounces of it. Street value = a lot more than we'd ever seen in our lives. The older, wiser, seemingly cooler guy knew what my best friend had; we did not. A deal was struck where in essence, Winky was given in trade a lot more weed in an exchange for the crack in a deal that was pennies for dollars. Keith was pissed.

The time surrounding this moment was a pivotal period within my mind and being, not because I benefitted financially from Copper's haul, but because I saw some new possibilities that were intriguing to me. Having now laid eyes on a different, more serious type of dope in large quantity, I felt it was time for my ascent into dope dealing hero-hood. It was time for me to live into my new identity. I was getting money directly from my dad in child support once per month. I saw an opportunity to go all in and try to be the dope guy, just like my idol Jon. Not only did I like the idea of being such a guy, but I also had a deep love for getting high, and due to my acne, which continued to worsen, my ego and my self-image desperately needed a confidence boost. Quickly, I became a pimple faced legend in my own mind, and a rather unsuccessful drug dealer, without a car.

Isn't it true that every teenager needs an identity of their own, and someone to base it off of? It was true for me. Prior to trying to root my identity as the dope guy, I was an athlete. I was blessed with my dad's athletic ability and most of his size (Dad 6'6", Namesake Jabe 6'8", me 6'3".) Once, during my freshmen year of high school in a county recreation basketball league that took place after school season ended, I showed up slightly a buzzed and scored twenty-seven points in the first half of a game. The beloved rec director at that time reminded me at halftime that I only needed sixteen more points to break the all-time Pulaski youth record for the most points in a game, which had been set by another hero. I already knew what was before me as they put the records on the schedules each year. I needed no reminder. My dad, the coach, knew too.

We were winning by so much in the second half, in his wisdom, he saw to it that I barely played. I scored thirty-seven and could've easily scored fifty that game (disclaimer: the opponent's two best players weren't there that night). I resented Coach dad for it at the time, but now I am thankful that he did what he did. I don't think my ego could've sustained the inflation.

The year dad sat me when I could've obtained county league "legend" status (sarcasm intended, as there are no such things as youth county league legends), we went on to go undefeated that year, and I shared the MVP award with two of my best non-Alum Spring area friends, Roger and Jason. When summer rolled around many of us who hooped for the high school loaded up to go to a varsity team camp at Catawba College. The best player on the team and I spent a good portion of the camp stoned.

I went to Catawba knowing, and without telling the varsity coach that I would be academically ineligible my sophomore year. That was the end of my basketball career as a player. That was the only hard discipline I received from any source during this stage in life, and it hurt. The discipline didn't really change anything, even though it stung.

Forget what I said earlier about no regrets and such because of the moments of now. I wish I would've made the grades necessary to keep playing basketball. I did have a chance my senior year. After some summer workouts and realizing how out of shape I was, I didn't, even though I could have with just a little initiative and effort. In terms of achievement, apathy was my greatest enemy, and most utilized character trait in those days.

One ending led to new beginnings. After my athletic career came to a screeching halt, I started buying ounces of pot, often delivered through the exquisite gate at the property where mom and I lived by an eccentric character in an old Duster. I would buy an ounce of pot, weigh it out in thin plastic sandwich bags using carburetor scales in 8th of an ounce increments. The price I paid for an ounce was too high, but it was what it was. Typically, my friends and I would smoke as much as was sold by any of us from any of our stashes. But we never went without. On occasion, Jon or some other older friend would come through with a good deal and I could make a little more money to buy a special treat, like a half-gram of cocaine or some mushrooms or LSD.

It was Matt and Jon's mom who, unbeknownst to me, was listening on the other line of the phone as I orchestrated someone meeting me up above their house in a church parking lot to sell a half-quarter of pot (a.k.a. an 8th). On the phone, I had at one point said, "Are you sure you don't want a quarter as opposed to a half-quarter?" As we returned from the deal in the parking lot, she met me at the door and screamingly reiterated the question she heard me ask on the phone. *"Are you sure you don't want a quarter as opposed to a half-quarter?"* It didn't sound too good or cool when she said it. I was forced to leave.

In the meantime, as I trudged back home red-faced, my mom (now tipped off) had moved one of the ceiling tiles in my room to discover a quarter-pound of pot stashed up there. She was furious and heartbroken. I convinced her that I had to sell all of it because it had been fronted to me and if I didn't pay the guy back, I might get hurt. That was lie, but it worked. I kept my weed, and my devastated mom made me vow not to get in this situation ever again.

It wasn't long after that incident that Matt's parents kicked me out again. I was sitting in the floor of Matt's bedroom, sort of curled up in a ball as Matt was lying on the bed choking on his own vomit after he and I went riding through town in a late-model sedan with a friend named Jamie and his dad Pete. As we cruised various backroads throughout Pulaski County, Matt drank more than his fair share of a handle of cheap vodka and orange juice chaser before we returned to his house. When Matt's parents busted into his room at the sound of him gagging, I couldn't help but laugh, even though without intervention he would have soon been dead, choking on orange vomit. There he was, jovial just a short time prior, now white as a ghost in his face with a bubbling orange ooze struggling to leave the corners of his mouth. Despite the scariness of the moment, no matter how hard I tried, I couldn't stop my hysteric laughter.

I swore to his parents then, and I say now, I didn't think it was funny, I was just a little drunk and didn't know what else to do. They threw him in the bathtub and me out the door. On that night, Matt's dad drove my drunken teenaged self to the basement apartment where I was once again greeted by my informed mother. I probably went inside after the drop off and made another vow. Living the life of a juvenile delinquent always involves jumping through some type of hoop or another, and making promises that you know you are never going to keep.

8

Hard

As crack (cocaine mixed with baking soda, cooked up until it becomes hard so that it can be smoked) became increasingly prominent in Pulaski, and in my friend network, I became sort of close to my friend Jason's brother Chris. Chris was "the man" and everyone knew it. In those days, with the crack, (a.k.a "hard") there were several guys who were "the man". Chris was by the far the nicest and most genuine of all of those I knew. He was a couple years older than me and had been in and out of school, and had already spent time in jail.

After Chris had been indicted on some drug charges, the Pulaski PD kicked in the door of the family's home while he, Jason, their little brother, and their mother slept inside. The door kicking was unnecessary, Chris was not that kind of threat to them. They could have just knocked. I think a lot of Pulaski P.D.'s anger and methods in those days had to do with the "this is war" mindset that Nancy and Ronald and some other politicians before them had initiated and perpetuated. Words create worlds, and "war" means "war" and war brings with it, aggression.

Chris did his bit in the lockup. It wasn't long after he got out that we started to hang out on a regular basis during my junior year of high school. He liked me and I liked him. He quickly trusted me enough to sell to me and that is how I got involved with crack on a larger level. I would get from Chris a "block." A block was 2.5 grams of crack. I paid $100 for a block. I could sell two half-grams or one gram of crack to some kids that were a year younger than me, or some fiend who was hanging around the porch at Chris' house and get my money back. That would leave 1.5 grams for me and whatever friend was with me at the time to smoke. We would break up the crack into smaller pieces and mix it in with some pot to smoke a creation known as a "woo" or a "wooly." This was the preferred way of smoking for many of us who were younger and desiring not to be labeled as crackheads. Crackheads smoked it straight, and that was looked down upon, stigmatized. Woolies were ok though, even for someone like Chris. It amazes me how quickly my mind would justify the next move down the ladder into a type of using that I swore I would never partake in. Each successive step down into the abyss of my addiction was always accompanied with "at least I'm not doing. . ."

The revolving $100 a day deal went on and on for a few months. Occasionally, I would get too high from smoking the woolies to go home. So, I didn't. Mom would be worried, but thanks to the technology of pagers, she could find out where I was, or at least where I said I was, when I called her after she paged me. The same pager came in handy for answering the young kid's calls for more dope. I call them young kids, because in my mind at that time they were. To be clear, they were only a grade behind me, but in my blurred, disillusioned perspective of myself, they were childish amateurs in this game of dope in Pulaski County.

A page would come in, often from one of the younger kids, I would find a pay phone, insert a quarter into the slot and call whoever was beeping me, letting them know where they could find me if they had $50 to get high on. I had a beeper and a gold chain around my neck (that my mom had bought me as a gift.) I was that legend in my own mind, but now with some credibility.

One night, Chris and I had been partying together just the two of us. We decided we would go see his cousin up on Case Knife Mountain. He and I hitched a ride up there. While there, I ate a handful of Xanax and washed them down with a forty-ounce Olde English malt liquor. All of this on top of a day of smoking woolies. I'm not sure why I decided to leave at 2:00 in the morning but I did. It was not long after Chris and his cousin passed out that I set out on my dazed sojourn across the entire town of Pulaski, to the edge of Alum Spring Rd.

I made it home sometime before the sun came up, urine that at some point had been running down my leg, now cold and drying, with fuzzy recollections rattling inside of my head regarding my long walk. This would not be the first or the last time I would blackout as a teenager. When I saw Chris the next day, he laughed heartedly and said, "Where the hell did you go in the middle of the night, Jabe Largen?" He often called me by my first and last name. I did not tell him or anyone else about my accident. Those who are legends in their own mind cannot be known as a pee-pee pants boy.

Around the time that Matt received his driver's license I got my hands on some quality psychedelic mushrooms. I was terrified as Matt drove us down Route 11 in his silver, early 90's model Mercury Sable. As we passed by the "barn" feed store, it felt like the car was hovering over the road. It felt as if we were about to take off flying through the air at any point. I screamed in terror for Matt to make it stop. With sweat rolling off of his forehead, jaws clinched and his knuckles white, he screamed at me to calm down, it was taking all his focus to keep us on the road. I forget who the other two were in the vehicle with us that trip, but I remember their laughing, indicating they were having much more fun than Matt and me.

That night, we made our way to Chris's. I sold him a small bag of mushrooms. It was his first time going on a psychedelic trip. We hung out and smoked some dope, and then Chris lost it. Totally, lost it. Eyes as big a saucers, and a perplexed look on his face, he took off and hid inside of the house refusing to come out. After waiting him out for about thirty minutes, we left.

The next day, sitting on his porch he tried to describe what the experience was like. He was half amused and half terrified as he explained his experience in an out of body way. He said, "Jabe Largen, I was walking around the house, and I could see my mom and then I could see myself. I tried to talk to her and me, but no words would come out. The reason was, I was dead."

A year or so later, Chris was recruited by a friend of his to go and try and to recover some money the friend had lost in a drug deal from an out-of-towner who was shacked up at the Washington Square Apartments, apartment 434. For whatever reason, Chris took a bb gun pistol with him to intimidate the man. Witnesses said Chris threatened to pistol whip the guy with the bb pistol. Chris was unaware that the man was armed with a real gun. As Chris was presenting the bb gun, a witness in the room was reported as shouting, "No, Chris! No!"

Chris was shot through the vital organs in his upper body. His body fell through the doorway, out onto the cold concrete stoop. He was taken to the hospital where he was later pronounced dead. Droves of people showed up at the ER in a scene that some described as an angry mob, some yelling, some crying, as Chris' body lay lifeless on the inside.

Chris was so loved in the community. The mob formed in part out of anger due to an out-of-towner being the one who slayed him. Justice was wanted. With that said, the mob formed more so out of love I believe. That love gave away to heartbreak and frustration as word spread throughout the crowd that nothing more could be done to save Chris's life.

In the church we call what the crowd did "lament."

A week or so later, I hopped in a Blue and White cab during a sleet and snowstorm and rode to pick Michael up on Snider Lane prior to going to Stevens Funeral Home. We stood outside the cab and smoked a joint, while the meter ran. Chris' casket was open. He looked just fine, but his breath was gone. I don't know if what he experienced those months before when he saw himself walking around the house dead was a premonition or not. It doesn't matter. A good human died for no good reason; he was nineteen.

It was a sad Winter in Pulaski. A lot of people really liked Chris; I was just one of many. A few years later Winky would move into Apartment 434. There were faded blood stains on the concrete outside of the door. I stepped over the bloody visage of my friend every time I visited.

9

Paw-Paw Part Two

CHRIS AND I WERE friends, not just acquaintances, but we were nowhere near being best friends. My best friend died the year before Chris.

Paw-Paw Largen was diagnosed with lung cancer, and there was no treatment that could help; none he was willing to subject his body to anyway. They brought in a medical bed for him as his body began to fail. The bed was set up in the living room of their home. He was ordered not to smoke any more Doral's, as each puff would take more and more time away from his earthly journey. When he could get away with it, he would sneak one in the bathroom, as if Maw-Maw couldn't smell it! On a few occasions, he got bold and snuck out of the house and jumped in his old brown truck to ride around and smoke. He was in no shape to drive, but he was determined. His stubbornness and outlaw behavior made me giggle, while it terrified the rest of the family. I imagine anyone he met on the road was terrified as well. On more than one occasion I fetched him his stash, tucked away in a brownish-gold soft pack with red trim, and stood watch as he went to the bathroom to smoke. After all, every outlaw needs a good lookout, and it was safer than his being on the road.

Eventually, his body deteriorated to the point that he had to be hospitalized. In those days, it was common in Pulaski for the hospital to serve as a place for a body to go and die. So, it was for James Alford Largen. He traded in his home hospital bed for the real thing, and it was clear he was not coming out once he went in.

I should have visited him more, but I was wrapped up in getting high. The night he died I was in a trailer park off Route 11 getting wasted with some friends from school and some adults I had known since childhood.

My father told me Maw-Maw was laying in the hospital bed with him when he passed. My mom tried to get in touch with me through my pager, but I ignored her. Eventually, I was tracked down through her getting in touch with one of the parents of one of the friends I was with. I had never felt so ashamed. Everyone in the trailer that night, although high as kites, showed great compassion as I found out the news.

Everything after finding out Paw-Paw had died was a blur, until I walked into his and Maw-Maw's house and saw my dad. My head hit his chest like a ton of bricks being dropped from a second story window. This was my first real experience with the death of someone I loved, and it was the death of the dearest person to my heart. And I had failed to be around. So much sorrow, so much guilt, I was overwhelmed. Maw-Maw did that sweet thing that grandparents are wired to do, she begged me not to cry, as Paw-Paw would not want to me to cry. "Yeah, but he is dead," I thought.

Eventually, my tears stopped, and I asked of Maw-Maw, dad, and my Uncle J.W. a question they were not expecting in that moment, the night of his death. "Did he tell you all where the money is?" They were all dumbfounded. They knew of no money. A year or so prior, Paw-Paw took me into his room to show me a lock box buried deep in the little closet he and Maw-Maw shared. Inside the lockbox were envelopes. One envelope for each of us there that night, and one for J.W.'s daughter Ashley. Inside of each envelope were five crisp $100 bills; flea market money from the year I was born, Paw-Paw had said. He told me that day that it was my responsibility when he died to make sure that everyone got their envelope. I was far more trustworthy, and we were far closer to one another when he told me as opposed to when the day of his death came. To further prove this point, between the day he told me of the money and the day of his death, I had stolen $100 out of Maw-Maw's envelope to buy drugs.

The night that Paw-Paw died I went into the bedroom closet and found the lock box and handed everyone but absent Ashley their envelope. The pain on Maw-Maw's face was obvious when she realized her envelope was less than everyone else's. My dad said, "Maybe he made a mistake mommy." She knew what happened, but she never said a word.

I should have not mentioned the envelopes that night. It was not the right place or right time. I should not have taken Maw-Maw's money either, but that was done. Younger me, in the moment thought, I should have taken all the money since no one else knew. That would have kept the grief in the room that night where it belonged, solely focused on Paw-Paw's death, and not additionally on who I had become. Was it the case that younger me was so far in the grip of addiction that I would twist (for my own self-interest) regretting that I had not taken all the money to avoid their experiencing the harm of the realization that I took part of it? Or was it from a place of genuine compassion? Probably some of both.

Within a week, the Largen family and all our extensions gathered into the chapel at Stevens Funeral Home for my Paw-Paw's viewing the night before he was to be buried (this sequence was the customary practice for most in those days). When I walked into the chapel and made my way down the aisle to his casket, I crumbled in the floor before his lifeless body. There he was. Callous hands folded upon his chest.

I will never forget the look of shock and horror on the faces of some of my family gathered there. What they did not understand then, and what I did not understand for years is that I fell there before his casket in agony; not just in grief, but also in guilt.

10

Almost

The dope shenanigans continued throughout high school. I had my regular gang of brothers, but I also had a whole plethora of other playmates. I skipped a lot of school with two such accomplices, Stoney and Darren. One day, after getting good and toasted we went to do something that for many youths in Pulaski County was a rite of passage: jumping off of the Lighthouse Bridge into Claytor Lake. We parked down by the lake on the backside of the store where Paw-Paw and I would often fish for those boney bites of brim. We sprinted up to the bridge (after all this is illegal, like most of our activities) and one by one we plunged. It was quite a rush watching the water get closer and closer. It was a rather refreshing and exhilarating plunge and rise to be honest.

After the jump, the three of us swam back to shore and rested. While seated on a concrete pier, Darren came up with what sounded like a great idea to stoned teenagers. "Let's swim back to the other side of the bridge and try to sink those buoys." Off we went. At this stage in life, we were fully bought in to the idea of destruction; of self, and of anything else with the potential to be.

Of course, buoys, by their very buoyant nature, cannot be sunk, and we soon lost interest. As I got to the edge of the bridge that was closest to shore, I realized something. I was exhausted. My companions were getting near the shore, and I remained very far away. I fought like hell to grab ahold of the moss-covered concrete pillars of the bridge beside me. The pillars were so slick, all I could grab a hold of were tiny little rocks that made up part of the massive concrete structure. All the effort exerted trying to cling to the pillar left my body feeling far more exhausted.

It became clear at that point, under that bridge, where I had fished as a child, and jumped as a teenager, that it was time to either swim or die. I made it about fifteen yards when I gave out again. This is when the bobbing started. I would go down into the lake, water above my head and back up again, head back above water; time and time again, each time head a little lower in both directions. As this was happening, Darren sprinted back up to the bridge and jumped in. He did so on probably my fifth time going down. I may have been able to manage seven or eight before not coming up. He placed me on his back and powered me to shore. Had Darren not done what he had done, I would have died that day.

After several of minutes catching our breath on the shore, we rode back to the school. We smoked another joint. I found no pleasure in it. To be honest, I never liked weed to begin with. You know, you can drown smoking that stuff.

It would not be long before the next near-death experience. About the time my Paw-Paw died, Michael got his driver's license. He was working at the now-closed Kroger grocery store in town to cover his cost of gas and to pay his share of the vehicle insurance. The vehicle was a Ford Probe. An almost sleek and sporty car with a manual transmission.

The Kroger job also allowed him to steal multiple bottles of Mad Dog (MD) 20/20. A true wino's wine. Michael would pick us up every morning after a Kroger shift to take us to school, along with a bottle of MD 20/20 for each of us. The Mad Dog provided a quick and ferocious intoxication, and if you were able to keep the wine down, it would make the first couple of hours of school entertaining (or so it seemed).

It was not the MD 20/20 that almost killed us however (although a few times it felt as if it might). What almost killed us was the Probe, or more accurately, Michael's driving of the Probe. One Saturday in the late 90's, our driver, Adam, Winky, and I had been on the search for a buzz. The plan was to go and solicit a beer purchase from Keith and Michael's former neighbor who was slightly older than us. As we headed down one of the roads that eventually connects to Alum Spring, Michael felt it fun to drive on the wrong side of the two-lane road. We made it through the portion of road that contains a ninety-degree curve and then began our descent down into a long straight away. As we sped down the wrong side of the two-lane, Adam and Winky did not seem to mind this maneuver as much as I did. I yelled angrily at Michael to stop being a "reckless asshole" and to get back in the right lane.

After my tirade, Michael spotted a dead possum or groundhog or some other unfortunate creature that serves as roadkill in those parts, lying flat dead on the double yellow lines separating the two-lane. To appease my desires to get back in the other lane, and in an attempt to further flatten the roadkill, Michael swerved so quickly and sharply that all control was lost of the vehicle. The last thing I saw before my eyes closed initially was a roadside bank rapidly approaching. The next time I opened my eyes we were in mid-air and almost upside down. All I could see was the field on the other side of the fence behind the roadside bank. We came to an abrupt stop. Expecting we were in the field at this point, eyes still closed, I silently said within myself, "Either I am dead, or one of them is."

My eyes opened. My vision was blurry, like one of those channels on the television used to be when you did not have strong enough rabbit ears or an antenna to get that channel. All that was in view were just little white and black dots dancing around frantically. The first thing I saw clearly was Adam in the passenger seat with his arms stretched out bracing his weight on the glove box. Winky was to my right behind Adam, he had his left arm wrapped under my right. I was holding on to the outer edges of the driver's seat in front of me. Michael's head was slumped over. His noggin slowly rose, I saw a lot of blood. He had broken his nose. Glass was everywhere. Michael said, "What happened?" "You about killed us, you dumb motherfucker" I replied.

The woman in the little house on the other side of the road phoned 911, "There are dead teenagers laying all over the road," a first responder classmate told us she had said on the dispatch call. We were not dead, but in the woman's defense, all four of us were laying in the road trying to regather our bearings.

My mom came and got Winky, Adam, and I when we refused to go in the ambulance. We dropped Adam off to his relieved, but angry mother. After much begging, mom bought Winky and I some wine coolers and we spent the evening shooting pool and picking out glass. It wasn't nearly the buzz we set out to find that day. Buzz or no buzz, the Probe was totaled, completely smashed, and I was grateful that my prediction of at least one of our being dead was not true.

11

Potential

THE CRACK PHASE FADED when mom and I moved one town over to Dublin (still a part of Pulaski County) my senior year. The house there was a nice little ranch two-bedroom, one-bath home with a carport that protected the landlord's 1965 and a half model Mustang. The home also had a large yard with an ancient and spectacular looking weeping willow tree. I was over the moon excited when I discovered the house was also built with a partially finished basement that would house my pool table.

My friends and I, the Alum Spring Rd. clan, and others like Jason, spent a great amount of time shooting pool or playing ping pong in the basement. I had a goal of lining the walls of the finished part with a-floor-to-wall empty beer can pyramid. We actually accomplished the feat more than once, after having been forced to tear down the first masterpiece. Apparently, there was an odor. Having spent a few years snorting substances up my nose, I couldn't tell.

It was about half-way through my junior year that my math teacher told me that I stood no chance of graduating on time. In a very short amount of time, I had gone from an honor's student to not graduating on time. My math teacher, and most teachers at Pulaski County High School, cared for me a great deal and always talked of my "potential." I used to loathe that word, "potential." I heard it so often, and every time I heard it all I could think was that I could care less about my so called "potential," athletic or academic or any otherwise. Every time it was said to me, I would get ticked off and rebel harder. Looking back, it was my feeling of shame that made it hard for me to hear about what I "could" be, thus making me more prone to act out in unhealthy ways due to the ways I viewed how I "was."

My math teacher was right about the not graduating on time thing though. There was no chance unless I entered the PBD program. She outlined the PBD program for me and offered me the chance to enter it based off her recommendation. PBD stood for "Performance Based Diploma." It was a nice way of saying, "We are going to give you a diploma so you can graduate when you are supposed to, so we don't have to deal with you anymore." One of the basic tenets of the PBD program was that all of us in the program were going to be entering the workforce immediately; many of us out of necessity due to having kids to feed or having no other means of support except oneself. Many of the program's participants had failed a grade in elementary school and needed to catch up for that reason.

Others had gotten into severe disciplinary trouble in high school for fighting, drugs, or bringing weapons to school and missed entire years, thus needing the program to graduate. Fights were common among those in the PBD program, especially amongst those who were there due to missing entire years of school for fighting. I stayed out of the way. To my knowledge, I was the only one in the program who was there simply because of prolonged apathy.

The PBD classrooms were in the math department part of the high school. We PBD students and teachers had two rooms within the math pod. One classroom for language arts, and the other for mathematics. We would spend half the day in one, and half the day in the other. Math and language arts were the only two subjects. The curriculum consisted of computer programs on WICAT computers, fully equipped with two types of floppy disk ports. The coursework was on a middle school level. In fact, I had already done the coursework on computers just like these when I was in the 6th grade. In PBD, I burned through the work with a speed our teachers had never seen before.

I finished all I needed to do to graduate in a couple of months. That left over a year of high school to just hang around. My senior year I would leave each day at 10:30 in the morning if I had a ride. Usually, an old friend named Justin from youth group, who I also played baseball with would give me lift. I couldn't get my license because my grades were so bad the school could not provide me a letter to show the DMV that I had earned the right to drive yet. Most of my time at school, regardless of if I had a ride or not, were spent helping Mrs. Trivette, the PBD language arts teacher. Mrs. Trivette loved me deeply. She had genuine concern for me, but never let that concern be expressed in a way that overwhelmed me. With her, there was never any talk about "potential," she would instead say things like, "you know, you are really smart." I liked the sound of that better.

She was diabetic and often had spells. I (of all 1,700 enrolled PCHS students) was granted daily access to the teacher's lounge to get her a Coke when needed. I was trusted to run errands for her regularly, even on the days when her blood sugar was normal. I don't know that she needed me to do any of these errands. I suspect she gave me these assignments to prevent me from becoming bored, but also to give me a sense of purpose and importance; to let me know I was trusted. She was probably also tired of watching me take everyone else's lunch money during our free time by cheating in games of five-card draw.

Mrs. Trivette was in her second marriage at this point. Previously, she had been married to another teacher, Mr. Hillman. She talked of Mr. Hillman with a teenage like sense of love and awe. They had been adventurers together. Each had hundreds of skydive jumps under their belts. One day, while enjoying time on the water together, Mr. Hillman drowned. There is no doubt, when he died that day in her presence, some of my beloved teacher died as well.

She did move on though, her natural free-spirited self could not be completely overtaken by tragedy. She would establish a scholarship for Mr. Hillman to be given through the school each year in his memory. In my final semester of high school, long after the scholarship application deadlines had passed, she approached me and asked what I thought about going to community college. I told her I had thought about it and figured that is what I would do. "I want to give you my husband's scholarship to help pay for it," she said. I was shocked, overwhelmed, grateful, loved. I would be the only PBD participant going to college that following semester, perhaps the only straight out of high school to college student in program history. I would do so with the help of someone who believed in me when I did not have the ability to believe in myself. Such a belief can be transformational, even if it is not realized immediately. One Mrs. Trivette can have a tremendous impact on the lives of students. And not just in the life of the student, but in the life of the student's family and through generations.

As we gathered in the gym one afternoon, the reaction of my graduating class at the scholarship awards ceremony was a giant gasp as Jabe Largen was announced as a scholarship recipient. In a graduating class of 430, I was #415 in terms of GPA. Most people knew who I was, and was I was about quite well. My deviance was no secret. Mrs. Trivette had a glisten in her eye as she greeted me after walking off the stage, having accepted my scholarship certificate.

Prevenient grace is what we of the Methodist persuasion call it; that is grace active in the life of one who has no knowledge of said grace existing or at work. No shortage of prevenience in my life. Vessels of God's grace such as Jean Trivette, poured into me continuously, long before I ever sensed it.

We graduated on a Friday night. Well, Adam, Winky, Matt, Michael and I did. Keith did not make it. I did not make it to the graduation party that my friends went to. They would throw down at a cabin in a nearby county owned by another friend's family. I had been to the cabin before for a night of trauma and near tragedy. That previous trip, after heavy drinking, Winky and I had just come back down from a mountain that we had inched up bit by bit thanks to the four-wheel drive capability of his *Suzuki Samurai*. When we made it back down and into the clear, Winky gave the steering wheel of the Samurai a quick jerk as we were travelling about twenty-five miles per hour (no roadkill involved this time) and we went tumbling.

Those back at the cabin said that when we rolled, they just saw headlights in the sky, and then none, then headlights in the sky, then none, and one more time the same. We finally came to a stop and Winky's body was on top of mine as we came to rest on the passenger side of the vehicle. I cussed at him a fair bit, and he and I pushed and clawed on each other as we attempted to exit through the driver side window.

When we made it back to the cabin having been rescued from the field by our concerned brethren, Winky sobbed for a solid hour. He was terrified that his father was going to kill him. At that point in the festivities, I would have allowed it, having just about tasted death in a meaningless fashion in some field far, far away from Alum Spring Rd. By the end of the night, compassion and forgiveness overtook me. I was glad he was, and would remain, alive.

Graduation night I was not invited back to the cabin. A month prior, Winky and I got into a fight at the cabin owner's house in Dublin. It all started on the deck surrounding the family swimming pool. My girlfriend attacked Winky. I, not fully understanding the context of what was going on, jumped on Winky, who did little to fight back. As that broke up (with Adam's help) my girlfriend and Wink's girlfriend fought on; both inside of the house and outside of the house, and down the basement steps they tussled. All the fighting was my girlfriend's fault, as was most violence around my life in latter high school. She had a knack for knocks.

After all the raucous was seemingly over, I hit our host in the nose for saying something I did not want to hear as we stood on his carport. Hitting your host in the nose is a good way not to get invited back to their cabin. Later the police showed up at mom's Dublin house to inquire about the incident. I denied hitting anyone, especially the host in the nose. The police didn't believe any of it, but they left.

In response to being left out of the cabin trip, I talked my mom into buying me a keg of Miller Lite to have at the house in Dublin. There were several keg parties at the Dublin house, however, this would be the first without my core group of friends. It was mostly without anyone outside of a half or dozen schoolmates. It was sad.

It was at the Dublin house that I got to know our neighbor Randy quite well. One day, shortly after moving in my senior year, Winky and I were smoking a joint on the carport, beside the homeowners antique *Mustang*. Suddenly, a voice from across the way says, "You guys mind sharing that?" It was Randy, talking to us from his kitchen window. Randy was probably in his late 20's or early 30's at this point. He had a good job, two young children, and was recently divorced. His love of drugs, and my love of drugs, made us friends quickly. Randy had a good cocaine hookup, and I had good hookups for everything else, and his job paid him well. I benefitted from our friendship.

One night at one of the Dublin keg parties (pre-graduation night), Randy met my mom. They hit it off and eventually started seeing one another. It was an awkward arrangement no doubt. Prior to my graduating on that Friday night, mom had moved in next door with Randy. I wasn't mad about it, nor do I have any negative feelings about it now. It was, as I said, just awkward. I certainly did not mind living almost completely unsupervised.

The Monday after graduating high school, my dad rode to Dublin to pick me up at 6:30 in the morning. We made a stop at the Hardee's in Dublin for a biscuit, and then we headed to the furniture factory. Dad was the manager of the Sand Room there, while my Paw-Paw Fisher worked in Finishing. I went to work in the Parts Inspection department beside my dad and his team in the Sand Room. My dad was a great manager, and his people loved him. I liked working in Parts Inspection. It was easy work, and often it was done around a large table with other people I could talk to. I was banking $6 per hour. Two of the people around the table that I worked with made the same wage and drove over an hour from West Virginia for it.

I couldn't understand why. I also wonder, what do they and their children and grandchildren do for a wage now?

Once that first post-graduation summer was over, I would be able to have flexible hours so I could go to community college. Dad had worked that arrangement out with Doug, the plant manager. I started to think, maybe adulthood was what I needed to fill my voids, and maybe even help me to fulfill my "potential". The year was 1999. I still lacked the understanding of how addiction worked, and how far I was already into it. Soon, I would learn.

12

OC's

It was during those early months at the furniture factory that dad and I really reconnected. We would often sit in the truck together and share lunch in those early months. We also continued to stop by Hardee's on the way in. Eating together and just being together brought us closer, even if a lot of words were not exchanged. It was also during those early months at the furniture factory that another great love in my life began to blossom, my love of pain pills.

In high school, I had snorted plenty of narcotic pain pills, especially in the latter couple of years. It was around my senior year when Oxycontin really began to make a splash in our area. In our county, we were experiencing an opioid epidemic in the late 90's and early 2000's. The national conversation about an opioid epidemic did not begin until many years later, when rich people and their children started dying in places far from Appalachia. We had been burying people for years by that time.

I remember the first time I snorted an "OC," as we called them (we called them "beans" as well). I was in the same apartment complex where Chris had been killed, at an older friend's apartment. I had doubts that the pill could live up to the hype. I watched as my older friend crushed the pill up on his kitchen counter. He cut it into a few lines, sniffed his line and handed me the straw for snorting. I yanked at it with all my might. Boy, was I wrong to ever doubt that this pill could be the real deal. It lived up to the dope fiend hype. It was a new type of pain pill high; it was a new type of high in general. Almost instantly, as the plastic straw departed my nose and the pill powder made its way through my sinus cavity and into the rest of my being, this pharmaceutical made me feel better than I had ever felt before.

OC's began to dominate my life. Not just my life, but the lives of almost all my friends, including the original Snider Lane, Veteran's Hill, Alum Spring crew. We were all still snorting them at the turn of the millennia, however, it would not be long before Keith would find his way to the needle. What our community quickly learned about these pills was regardless of how you took them, once you did, you were hooked. Popular shows such as *Dopesick* and *Pain Killer* do a good job of showing the devastation caused by the quick addiction, but what they leave out is the effect and prominence of the needle. (Perhaps the books the shows are based on, highlight the needle more effectively/accurately. Admittedly, I have not read either). Almost everyone I knew came to know the needle at some point. For this reason, and probably a few others, Oxycontin began to be called Hillbilly Heroin.

The doctors, the P.A.'s, the pharmacists, and the drug reps were all getting paid big bucks. The stockholders celebrated. Investment account holders rejoiced. The people we got our OC's from were getting them straight from doctors in quantities that made no sense. I remember one of our connections who would go to Roanoke to see the infamous Dr. Knox. He would come back with 180 OC 80's (the higher the number, the stronger the pill), 180 OC 40's, and 60 OC 20's. That was for one month. The 80's were the primary treatment. The 40's and 20's were offered for "breakthrough pain." If you were to take six OC 80's a day and require something for "breakthrough pain" you would have to weigh about 2,000 lbs. and be dealing with several gunshot wounds, terminal cancer, and a bad case of gout. It's just not humanely possible to require that much opioid medication.

Also, to add some different perspective, for street value, those three prescriptions, the main one and the two for "breakthrough pain" would be over $20,000 worth of dope in our community around the year 2000. Also worth mentioning, it's not like it was just one person getting that amount of dope from a doctor. There were hundreds of people, and dozens of doctors.

As shocked as I was to find out that such corruption was possible, I was equally as grateful it was. I had my own opportunity to receive prescriptions from a popular doctor's office in Dublin on the claim I had severe shoulder pain. I was 21. On my initial visit to this office, I was seen by one of the two Nurse Practitioners; the two of them were a husband-and-wife duo. Patients at this office had to work their way up to see the Doctor who owned the practice. It is kind of like leveling up in a video game until you get your turn with the boss. The male practitioner came in and saw me during this original visit.

The first impression he made upon me was by way of his breath; think rotten eggs. In all his rancidness, he asked about my pain, and where I was on a scale of 1–10 and he pushed and prodded on me a bit, and then he left the room. He returned a few minutes later with a printed-out version of my background check which did have some items on it by this point in life. He pointed to one of the charges and said, "Can you tell me about this." So, I told him. And then, he said something quite unexpected, "You know, there are a lot of people out there who would snitch on us if they thought it could get them out of trouble. We can't have that here."

"I'm not snitching on anybody."

He handed me my prescription with the Doctor's photocopied signature on the bottom. Long after I stopped using, the three of them at that practice were charged with different crimes related to their distribution of narcotics. No snitches were needed. The boss doctor received over 170 counts of criminal misconduct. She was sentenced to thirty-three months.

13

Regional

THE EUPHORIA OXYCONTIN OFFERED was unmatched. I could snort up a week's paycheck on a Friday night, along with my best friends, who were snorting up their paychecks on a Friday night. In our euphoric and stupefied state, we would sit around and try to look at, and talk to, one another as we nodded off to sleep. Throw in a half-gallon of Jim Beam, a stereo, and the pool table, and life was good; until Saturday, now broke, when we had to hustle our way to getting high again.

When the lease ran out on the Dublin house, mom helped me purchase a trailer in Draper (still in Pulaski County). There, I made several new friends. All were much older than me. Some who were good friends with my Uncle J.W., who also had a deep, abiding love for pain pills and alcohol among other things.

These new Draper friends would open so many new drug networks for me. Pain pills galore, along with a solid connection to the best cocaine around. My Draper trailer became a hotbed for drug activity, seven days a week.

It was no wonder that after one year of community college I quit. I felt terrible for dishonoring Mrs. Trivette and the scholarship, but the OC's had a hold on me that no feelings of guilt and shame could overcome. After dropping out, I got a job at the newly opened Dish Network call center in Christiansburg. It paid $3.50 an hour more than the furniture factory, which meant a paycheck could keep me high for at least two days. It didn't take long for me to move up the ranks at the call center. Then, it didn't take long for me to get fired for not showing up. I was firmly within the grip of the opioid addiction. All my time and money went into maintaining my habit, which ironically led to missing the work, which paid me the money I needed to get high. I missed one day too many and that was that.

It was at this point that many friends and/or associates were getting busted for possession, or possession with intent to distribute (a fine law that can be manipulated to turn a junkie into a kingpin in front of the judge). Others were targeted by informants to catch the biggest charges of distribution. I continued to dodge the major court cases during this stretch of life, with the exception of being charged multiple times with "Driving with no license" or "Driving on a suspended license." I accumulated 6 of those combined. I was headed to court on 9/11/01 to answer for a no license charge when the radio reported the first plane crashing into the World Trade Center. Aside from being horrified by the events in New York, D.C. and the Pennsylvania field, I was also grateful that in response to the events the courthouse had been closed.

Eventually, the courthouse reopened, and I was sentenced to serve weekends incarcerated at the regional jail for my 6th driving on a suspended license (the law said you were supposed to be jailed after your third and any subsequent offense). I ate a bunch of Xanax before going in that first weekend. I was excited when in the holding cell, unexpectedly, my old friend Keith came hop-skipping in. Through just being Keith, he kept me and the holding cell entertained prior to going into our block for the weekend each time. The block we were in was so overcrowded that all of us weekend guys had to sleep on the floor. Keith and I caught a hard time when everyone woke up to find Keith asleep with his arm draped across me after my first Friday night in. We were both so tore up from all we took prior to intake, we could care less.

In my experience on those weekends, I observed and experienced a few things of note. Importantly, those weekend lockups were the extent of my overnight incarcerations. There are many who can say so much more about life inside of correctional institutions. Some of them have said much more to me, and therefore also formed my thoughts on many things jail and prison. Additionally, held in tension with my experiences and the experiences of those I know, I have also been formed a particular way in matters of incarceration through my education.

With that said, in my experience there are few things more humiliating than intake, the shower, the cavity check, and the delice-ing that follows. You strip naked before an intake officer, bend over to prove you are

REGIONAL

not concealing any contraband, then take a cold shower, prior to being doused with a powder to kill any lice you may have.

After that embarrassment, you are given a "setup" which is your bed mat wrapped around some other necessity items you will need for your stay. You are looked at and analyzed by an officer who sizes you for the abrasive, cotton, striped jumpsuit that you are given. After sliding the jumpsuit on, you are pointed toward the stockpile of orange rubbery sandals to hopefully find your size. Once moved to and in your "pod" you settle in with your setup in any available space and then wait for the time to unfold.

The food was interesting. The best way I know how to describe it is gruel-like. For the record, I do not recall being served gruel, but based off the descriptions of it I have read, that's what we are going with to paint the picture. A liquid sort of consistency is present in all the items on the tray with the exception of the slice of white bread. It was brought to our tiny pod by inmates whose good behavior had earned them the right to be Trustees. Being a Trustee has its advantages, such as extra food, and the ability to get out of your pod for a few hours each day. The Trustees during my stay, many of whom I knew, would wheel in a 6-foot-tall warming cart jam packed with hard plastic trays that looked like they were made by the company your mom tried to get everyone to buy items from through her at a party in the 80's. The contents of the trays tasted as pleasant as eating your own hair.

The guys being held there for longer periods of time were grateful to see I had no desire for my gruel. To them it was as good as anything imaginable. The majority of those in our little unit were federal inmates who the government was paying the privatized jail a great amount of money to house as they awaited trial or awaited court appearances in which they were witnesses. There were some federal prisoners there who were already serving life sentences. For those folks, food was food, and it was as good as it was going to get. I had my girlfriend Amber waiting to bring me a delicacy on Sunday evening. A *Whopper* with cheese.

Unfortunately for the federal inmates, the regional jail lockup did not afford many of the same privileges as prison. This made the unit I stayed in extremely tense. For example, "yard" time was limited to once every few days, whereas those in the larger pods of incarcerated persons were granted daily access. One weekend, we were granted "yard" access, and the long-time inmates were thrilled. The Correction Officers (CO's) led us through winding hallways all separated by steel doors until we arrived just on the other side of one of the larger pods of fellow inmates. To my surprise, the yard was a tiny area, as sanitized looking as an operating room, and where I imagined grass, there was a rubbery looking concrete.

When we made our way back from the "yard" to our tiny pod, Keith spotted someone he knew in the tiny pod to our left. With their faces pressed to the small, eye-level window on their respective cell door, the two of them mouthed words to one another for several minutes. Keith was trying to update this non-weekend inmate of life on the outside. Keith repeatedly, to much of our pod's amusement, continued in a charade like fashion to tell this poor guy that his girlfriend has been doing "you know what" with some other dude while he had been locked up. Based on the guy in the other cell's anger upon realizing what Keith in his charades was saying, I imagined he would be coming back to the regional lockup soon after release.

Later that night, jailhouse ingenuity was on full display as I witnessed someone from that tiny pod to our left, cast a cigarette on a string from under their steel door to ours. The ragged looking cigarette was pulled through the bottom of our door, and the string released so it could be pulled back into the other pod.

Someone had managed to get a hold of some matches and four or five of the long-term guys puffed and cherished this single cigarette as if it were one of Cuba's finest hand-rolled being enjoyed after a five-star meal with a glass of bourbon in hand. Of course, items like cigarettes typically only come in through someone bringing them in concealed and somehow making it through the shower check at intake. Those of us in for the weekend in my pod were not fans of concealment, or the risk associated with it. The long-term guys were highly upset every weekend when we weekenders showed up with nothing stashed. "We need some better weekenders," one of them always remarked.

Mental health, addiction, and incarceration are the Trinity of Criminal Justice in the United States. If you are not sure what I mean by that, go spend a night in a block or pod and you will come to quickly learn. On the first weekend I served time, a tall, slim, dark shaggy-haired gentleman covered in scabs, was brought in on Saturday and placed in our unit. Aside from the hint that was his appearance, it was obvious from the jump he was struggling with his mental health. He would take into fits of screaming, followed by fits of quoting scripture in Spanish. Although, not Hispanic, he indeed knew the language. Me being me, I had to test him (I knew maybe all of 30 words or phrases). He passed (I think).

That second night in, I didn't have to worry about Keith's arm being draped over me as I laid in the floor. I couldn't sleep. I was too busy watching as the new inmate paced back and forth in the tiny bathroom area which I laid closest to, on the floor not far from the sinks.

The next day, some of the guys beat on the only door in and out of our confinement to get the attention of the CO's. The aim of this was to see about getting the guy out of our cell and getting him some place inside where he could get some help. The CO's laughed.

When I came back a couple of weeks later, the manic man was gone. I inquired if he got out, and then learned that he was still locked up, but now in a more protective, isolated environment. He had requested and been granted a pencil with which he stabbed himself repeatedly. Upon hearing the news of his self-harm and segregation, I felt an empathy and/or sympathy that was mostly foreign to me in those days. As awful as I felt my life was at that time, it was obvious there were those suffering far worse, and apparently through no choice of their own.

Recidivism is another sad reality of criminal justice in the United States. So long as there is an industrial prison complex, there will also be a high percentage of recidivism. A privatized prison industry can only turn massive profits if it has individuals incarcerated who's lodging, meals, and security are being paid for by the government (via taxpayers). So long as money is a motivating factor in keeping inmate numbers high, why would there be any real attempts at rehabilitation? Imagine how profitable and occupied a bar would be if they ceased selling alcohol and committed to only serving customers water for the betterment of their health. Likewise, there is a reason why most fast-food chains removed salads from their menus several years ago.

An example of this never-ending cycle of recidivism is Michael's brother Ricky. When I first met Michael, Ricky was in prison. He had been in there for quite some time. I remember the excitement when Rick finally got out and came back home to live with the family. It wasn't long after getting out that Ricky not only picked up his old habits, but also the illegal means he had used many times in life before to sustain said habits. It was the means that led to the multiple imprisonments. One day, in the asphalt driveway of their home, filled with loads of Xanax, forty-something year old Ricky cried, "I want to go home, I want to go home, I want to go home." When his mother did her best to convince him he was at home he replied, "Not here. To the penitentiary. I want to go home to the penitentiary."

Institutionalized. It wasn't long after that, Ricky got his wish. He stayed there for a bit, and when he got out again, he picked up where he left off the last time. Eventually the void swallowed him up and he died; overdose I was told.

14

Love

IN 2001, I BEGAN living with my friend Kevin in his single-wide, which was just down the road from the one mom helped me buy in Draper. Kevin's was a 60's or 70's model single-wide with the hitch still attached. Out behind the tin structure there was a glorious view of rolling pastureland about as far as eye could see. Like most of Draper, the land around our road had a paradisical quality to it.

I was forced to live with Kevin (or anywhere other than my home) because I did not pay my electric bill, and the service was cut off. I stayed with him for a few months, often in hunger. We both had the same problems, we loved pain pills, beer, and we had no jobs or money. We relied on the generosity of neighbors like Rocky and Bill to keep us going sometimes. These were tough times, but I would be lying if I said they weren't fun times. Fun being a subjective term of course.

As mentioned previously, we had a whole crew living in and around Draper those days. I say "we" because they welcomed me into their well-established community quickly and with open arms. I was grafted in. At that time, the Draper roaming ground was still theirs. I was the youngest of the Draper group by a good ten years. Most of the guys had been married at least once and divorced at least once. They were friends of biker gangs and lovers of inexpensive beer and high-quality cocaine.

It was a simple life outside of the hustle to keep things going. We feasted on bologna all the weeklong and partied all the weekend long, firing up a grill at someone's place and dining on such delicacies as frog legs and deer steak, while chugging ice cold Natural Light. The problem was our way of life was not sustainable for most of us, myself included. At my level of pill usage, shoving them up my nose was not sustainable either. To keep up with the habit, I had to start selling dope or stealing stuff. I am not a good thief, so I had to at least sell enough pills to keep myself going. Soon, I would have to start hustling for two.

Amber and I went to school together for the entirety of our adolescence. Her family lived in town, not far from the middle school we both attended in the early-90's. I was attracted to her at an early age, and in fact, we "went together" for a period of time in middle school. We would hang out at the YMCA during that period, early summer, some year or another, and play basketball and hold on to one another in the pool. We were both hyper-competitive, so the flirty sweetness stopped when we hit the hardwood. We would quickly make up by hugging it out in the pool. My older friend Jon's girlfriend at the time was Georgie, and Georgie was the lifeguard, and she made sure our holding only got so close.

Speaking of close, one-night Winky and I made our way to the New River Valley Fair. Upon arrival, there we see Amber who was snuggled up like a bug in a rug to someone I loathed. That was the end of our school-aged romance. I wasn't given much say in the matter to be honest. To this day, she remains bitter that I gave the handmade necklace or bracelet or whatever it was she made me to one of my friends. In my defense, what was I supposed to do? Use the jewelry as prayer beads to plead with God to return her to my arms? Yeah right. I mean, I even dedicated a song to her on Country 107.1 PSK one evening that summer. As we would say in those days, what she did to me "was dirty."

Amber thrived in high school, where I obviously did not. She was able to play basketball all four years, when I only earned eligibility for two. She got accepted to Virginia Tech to continue her education which she set out to do a couple of months after I started hand sanding and inspecting curio cabinet parts.

Our paths did not cross again until another summer, the summer of 2001. One night I was at Loving Field playing in the Men's softball league, just like the heroes of my youth. I was quite high on pills so I can't tell you how I played that night. I can tell you that an old friend of Amber and me asked if I wanted to accompany he and his girlfriend to the basement of Amber's parents' house, which had become her apartment of sorts since she began commuting to Virginia Tech. My response was something along the lines of "Hell yeah I do."

I rolled into Amber's basement that first night, having not been there since a middle school party where I served as part-time DJ, playing "Whoomp! There It Is" on repeat. Whoomp, there she was, sitting on the couch, as good looking as ever, slightly swaying while smoking a cigarette and cupping a cheap beer in a can. I had a pocket full of hydrocodone, that quickly emptied out as our noses filled up. It was love at first snort. I had suspected that she liked to get high, and my suspicions proved true. In fact, she was far more advanced in her usage than I had expected.

I slept on the basement couch that night and had breakfast with the family the next morning. Her mother said I reminded her of the guy who Amber rode the fair ride with all those years ago. It ticked both her dad and me off. We would stay ticked at each other, one or the other of us, or a combination of all involved for many years to come.

Ironically, our first real date after the post-softball game pill fest was to the Salem Fair. We did not snug up like bugs on rugs on any rides. We did take in an Aaron Tippin concert while there. I cannot say I remember one bit of it. I am sure he sang *Blue Angel* and the one about the radio working just fine. The pills and alcohol had us both on a good one. I do know that when we rolled back into Pulaski, my ex-girlfriend spotted us in the Food Lion parking lot near the pizza place I worked at, while we were getting more beer. She tried to fight Amber and thankfully that didn't happen. To be sure, there would have been blue lights and handcuffs for a lot of us, even the non-combatants.

I stayed the night with Amber again. The next morning, we woke up, took the top off her teal *Honda Del Sol* and went riding. The outlaw in me had been looking for a Bonnie I suppose. She had been looking for a well-connected Clyde. We found each other. The rest is, as they say, history. Or in our case, high-story.

15

Indictments

My dodging major charges ended in early 2002, or more technically in late 2001. My now-deceased friend Chris had a brother, previously mentioned, named Jason who I had also been close with. Jason and I played basketball together for several years. He was a frequent visitor and overnight stayer when mom and I first moved to the basement apartment. As we might have said in those days, we were tight.

In mid-2001, Jason had established a solid Oxycontin connection one county over, in Wythe County, with some family members who had a neighbor who was sitting on pills like Willy Wonka sat on chocolate. We would take the daily thirty-minute trip "up the road" to buy as many OC 80's as we could. We would get them for $50 a pop and then head home to sell them for $80 a pop.

I was working 3rd shift at the company my mom worked for and was bringing home a weekly paycheck of around $300 per week. That $300 would immediately be invested into six pills. All I had to do was sell four of the six at $80 to turn a $20 profit and get high for a day. The $20 profit would go to cigarettes for Amber and I, a few $1 chicken sandwiches from Burger King, and a splash of gas as we departed for the interstate toward Wythe County. Finally, those middle school honors mathematics classes were paying off.

Repeat the routine the next day, and so on and so forth for a handful of months.

One day we made the trip "up the road," and I got good and high as was my custom prior to going in for night shift at the coating plant. When I got off work that morning, I headed to Jason's apartment, also my custom.

As I nodded in and out of consciousness, Jason answered a call and informed me that Wayne was coming to buy a couple of pills from him, thus enabling us enough cash to head back "up the road" later that day.

Wayne was a full on badass. Nobody messed with Wayne. He had a head the size of a watermelon that looked like it was poured in concrete. His hands were the size of cabbages and looked as solid as a bone in ham. I did not know Wayne all that well, but we were acquainted enough, primarily through Adam. Wayne came into the apartment that morning and there was some minor b.s.-ing back and forth between he and Jason. Then, Wayne asked if he had any more pills to get rid of, in addition to those he originally came to get.

In my dazed state, I spoke up and said that I had "one and a half." Did I need to sell them? No. I already had enough money to go back up the road. Do I wish I held on to them? Yes. Wayne gladly took my one and a half, handed me $100 (a bargain) and started to head out. My only other recollection of that morning was Jason asking Wayne how he got there. We all knew he had no license, just like the rest of us. Wayne simply said, "My uncle" and headed out the door and down the metal steps toward the gravel parking lot underneath the elevated apartment.

A couple months later we found out it was not Wayne's uncle who had given him a ride that day. It was an undercover detective with the Sheriff's Department. The cigarette Wayne had tucked behind his ear that morning: a recording device. Allegedly, Wayne, having previously been caught stealing from Wal-Mart, had turned into a confidential informant to lighten the blow on his sentencing. There was also a rumor in those days that informants were getting paid per successful recording and transaction. The most I ever heard rumored was an amount just enough for the informant to go out and buy at least one pill. I'm not saying that is what happened in our case, I don't have any knowledge that it did. I'm just saying, I heard things like that were happening around that time and place.

When the indictments dropped late fall of 2001, Jason was listed, as were several other associates who we knew had also sold to Wayne. Missing from the indictment list, one 20-year-old named Jabe Largen. Figuring that Wayne had got Jason some time other than that morning I offered up my last one and a half 80's, I figured I had dodged a ginormous bullet. It wasn't until the local newspaper ran a story in January of 2002 that I found out that I hadn't dodged squat. My Maw-Maw Largen was the first to see it in the family. She let dad know, and through him, word got back to me. I had been deemed, "A Fugitive From Justice." Come to find out, the Sheriff's office came to serve me a warrant the same day they busted Jason and the others. The problem was, they went to the address of the single-wide in Draper, now occupied by an aunt. They couldn't have looked too hard for me; I, the unknowing fugitive, wasn't that hard to find. What was I supposed to do? Call the Sheriff's Office to make sure they didn't make a mistake when my name was not listed in the newspaper with Jason's a couple of months prior?

After the fugitive story in the paper ran, Jason (out on bail) and I went back "up the road," and I got good and high, then turned myself in. They loaded me up into a cruiser at the Sheriff's Office and transported me to the regional jail where I had done weekends in the privatized palace of recidivism. Much to my relief, I was released on my own recognizance having no prior record outside of traffic violations. Soon after my release, my mom hooked me up with a lawyer. I met him in a small office in an old building by the Wade's Supermarket near where mom and Randy lived. The little, balding, white-haired lawyer made no promises but was optimistic that if I had to go away, it would not be for long. My immediate thought after meeting him was that mom should have hired another lawyer.

One by one, Jason and my other friends/associates started going to their court dates. One by one, they received sentences that required them to be incarcerated for a minimum of one year. When my time came, my attorney struck a deal with the Commonwealth's Attorney. The whole agreement from my attorney's perspective was predicated on my lack of a serious criminal record and the fact that Wayne went to the apartment on that morning with intent to only buy from Jason. I, my lawyer argued, was an afterthought. Wayne had bragged a bit, calling me a "bonus two for one" on the wire recording once he got back into the detective's car.

Oddly enough, the transcript of the wire recording mostly read "Inaudible" for all of Jason's and my talking. We were so messed up and our speech was so slurred they couldn't make out what we said in transcribing the wire tape. Unfortunately, all they needed were dollar amounts and quantities, and those came through loud and clear enough by way of a fake cigarette tucked behind an ear.

The judge in my case accepted the deal and I was placed on probation, with all my jail time suspended on the condition that I complete probation and the VASAP program for drunk drivers. I was grateful, yet I still felt guilty that Jason was in jail. Come to find out, Wayne wore the wire on him more than once, resulting in a multitude of extra charges. Jason and I would reconnect a year or so later, when he got out of jail. By that point, he had acquired some phenomenal new contacts for all kinds of good dope. Funny how that happens. I have witnessed it more than once, where long stints in jail or prison become post-graduate places of education and connection for addicts.

As for Wayne, he assaulted me one day as I awaited a pill delivery at an older friend's trailer across from the New River Valley Speedway in Pulaski, County, near Radford. This older friend had also been popped by Wayne's wire that indictment season. Wayne had sent Adam and another guy there to cop dope for him since he obviously couldn't, being a freshly minted snitch. In fact, Wayne had snitched on the very guy he now needed dope from. Wayne was somehow triggered from afar as he waited for his dope. About 2 minutes into Adam and the other guy's arrival on his behalf, Wayne pulled up in the driveway and tried to fight my older friend. Everything that ensued was chaos and madness.

After my older friend grabbed a wooden baseball bat, Wayne retreated from him and turned his anger toward dope sick me. He grabbed me by the throat with one cabbage head sized hand and hit me in the side of the head with the other, saying that I "had been talking shit about his family." None of that was true. Eventually, Adam the peacemaker got him off me.

After taking care of my dope sickness, I went to the magistrate and took out charges on Wayne for assault. In an ironic twist of fate, he spent several days in jail, while I spent no time for the dope charge. When his court date came for the assault, I didn't show up, and the charges were dropped.

Although unplanned and unexpected, Wayne and I snorted coke together a few years later. No hard feelings. In those days we were all just sick people making perpetually bad decisions that led us further into a darkness that we did not have the power to emerge from on our own. No need for grudges once a power outside of yourself graces you with the ability to emerge into the light mostly unscathed. Jesus talked about stuff like that a time or two. He seemed to point to it being imperative that we listen.

I should have gone to prison. If not originally, then for violating my probation. The judge clearly said if I fail a single drug test my time would no longer be suspended. I failed the second one I took; the second one of only three. The stuff you can buy at GNC to clear your urine of illegal substances did not work that time, for the first time. I failed for morphine. Somehow, I never heard a word, even though for the duration of my probation I kept mumbling them. I have maintained that there was a miscommunication between one party or the other, or perhaps, I wore the system down with my pretending as if no test was ever failed.

As mentioned earlier, in this grace-filled existence, who really deserves what? And when? Why? And why is it that when what is "deserved" is levied, the levying is inconsistent from one reckoning or blessing to the next? Among us mortals, if anyone claims to know the answer to any of the above undoubtedly, I will without shame, run away from them as fast as I can. I'd encourage you to do the same.

16

Graduation

It was in the Draper days that I was introduced to another beloved friend who is now among the dearly departed, Hogg. Hogg was a local dope legend, and a hero of mine (If you haven't noticed already, I always loved as heroes those that most would deem as the bad guys. All my middle school book reports were on outlaws and gangsters, the likes of Jesse James, Billy the Kid, and Al Capone, to name a few.)

Hogg was one of the old heads, even though when I met him, he was only in his early thirties. To be in good with him meant that you were probably never going to be without, at least in terms of knowing where to get some OC's or something comparable. Amber and I were still just dating then, and she and I spent most of our dates hanging out at Hogg's, nearly all-day, every day.

This level of dope doing and dealing was higher than what I was used to, but I felt up to the challenge. I had been training years with the determination of an Olympic athlete for this. Hogg and I had many things in common, but a lot of things uncommon as well. One of the biggest things we had not in common was how we did our dope. Hogg used a needle, while I was a snorter. The more I watched him and his best friend shoot up, the more I wanted to try it. Their high was different than mine. It was faster, more intense, more technical.

One day, at Hogg's mom's house, in a little village constructed in war times for employees of an ammunition plant, it was just he and I. I begged him to work a pill up and to put it my arm. Hogg genuinely did not want to do it, knowing full and well that once I had my first shot, I would be chasing everyday thereafter. After his initial resistance, he said, "Oh fuck it, come here." In less than two seconds, the big guy found a vein, popped my skin with the needle point, pulled blood back through the plunger, and pushed the OC 40 through. My head went fuzzy, my body felt warm, I could taste the narcotic in a way that I never had before. This was it. This was the ultimate high. There are two things in life that I remember doing for the first time with an ultimate fondness: shooting dope and eating Mexican food. I went on chasing that first shot euphoria for a long time after that, one shot at a time. The needle was going to be my undoing, over and over again, until I was finally unraveled. No shot was ever as good as that first shot. All that followed was disappointment, consequences, struggle, and illness.

I would often drive Hogg to Roanoke where we had a few connections for lots of the OC 80's for half of the Pulaski County price. I don't ever remember the drive back. I do remember being in one house that we often frequented after making our connection and going into the room where the occupants of the house shot their dope. I'll never forget the blood splatters all over the ceiling and walls where the homeowners would rinse out their bloody needles by spraying the watery, bloody mix on anything solid. It was like unsanitary abstract art by the great Greco-Roman artist Hepatitis. Rightly, due to the blood splattered artwork, and the amount of shooting up that takes place, such rooms are known as "shooting galleries."

After that first shot from Hogg, I quickly learned to work the pills up and shoot myself up without any assistance. The process was far simpler than I had originally thought. There was an immediate payoff to shooting up that other methods of using did not have. The head would feel warm and fuzzy, especially across the brow. The body would fully relax, and the eyes would slowly close. After nodding out for a while, you could take what was left in the spoon and the cotton swab and work up what was called a "second shot." Far less powerful than the first, second shots were, more times than not, a futile attempt to go further into the nod than you already were. To the hole in my arm, and to my body's chemistry, the first shot had already done all that could be done to satisfy. It's kind of like going to eat at a Mexican restaurant and your food is brought out after you have already eaten three baskets of tortilla chips and salsa; already full, appetite satisfied, all else is waste.

In those early days, it certainly was "hit" or "miss" depending on how messed up I was, or how impatient I was. "Miss" was no fun. A miss is where the tip of the needle is not properly placed within a vein. After missing, abscesses would form and they would be big and painful and, although colorful in shades of blue, yellow, brown, and purple, they were not pleasing to the eye. A bad abscess could take weeks to heal. They were medically dangerous for a number of reasons as well. There was also another major inconvenience to a miss: the euphoric feeling of the shot would not be achieved.

It was the spotting of one my abscesses by my mom that led me to rehab the first time. I say rehab, but actually it was a seven-day trip inside a facility so I could start going to the Methadone clinic in a town called Galax, about forty-five minutes from Pulaski. This would be the first time my dad drove me to treatment and arranged to pay for my stay.

Galax is more well known to most for its bluegrass Fiddler's Convention as opposed to its Methadone. Methadone is a drug that was created by a couple of German scientists during the time around World War II. The hope was it could be a more effective and less addictive way to treat pain than Morphine (history has shown, they were wrong). Methadone's usage as an opioid treatment medication did not begin until many years later. I'm not sure when Methadone began being dispensed in Galax, but in the early 2000's I was grateful that it was, in the red syrupy form that I found it.

When I went into the Methadone clinic, Amber was pregnant, and I had been out of control in my using. It had not been long since I was indicted, and it was time to get help. The clinic seemed like the easiest, pain free way to do it, thus allowing me to become a good dad when the time came. That first rehab stint was quite the experience. I met people from all over the country who were just like me. Well, at least in their love of getting high. I met an airline pilot, a coal miner, a former college athlete, and handfuls of junkies who had no consistent workplace, just like me. Not surprisingly, all the folks there for Methadone treatment due to OxyContin addiction were from places in Appalachia, just like Pulaski.

The Methadone worked. I had no desire to shoot dope so long as I woke up on time to get my dose. Some days, thanks to the "treatment" medication I was able to feel higher than I could out scrounging and hustling to keep from being sick from a lack of opioids. All I had to do to feel good was to wake up, eat breakfast, drink something that tasted like cough syrup from a tiny plastic cup, go to a class, eat lunch, play basketball, go to a class, eat dinner, go to an in-house recovery meeting, go to sleep, repeat until the week of "rehab" was up.

To be sure, the stay there was much more enjoyable than my nights in weekend jail. As I was released back into the wild, I was convinced that

I was on my way to becoming a responsible and productive member of society. Thanks be to Methadone, the cheaper, legal, and more effective way of getting high, in the name of not getting high.

17

Miriam

A MONTH AFTER LEAVING rehab, we found out something was possibly wrong with Amber's pregnancy when the results came back from the twenty-week alpha-fetoprotein bloodwork. She and I loaded up and went to Roanoke to see a specialist who could help us to better understand what was happening. A large needle was inserted into Amber's stomach to retrieve some of the amniotic fluid that surrounded the baby in the womb. After that painful process, we headed to the ultrasound room filled with hope and joy.

I'll never forget the look on the ultrasound tech's face as she performed this enhanced imaging look at our baby girl. Eventually, we made our way out of that dark room and down a hall to a well-lit but closet sized office. Soon a prenatal doctor came in and told us that not only did the ultrasound show, but the amniocentesis confirmed, our child had a rare chromosomal defect known as Tri-somy 18. The more well-known Tri-somy disorder is Tri-somy 21, aka Down's Syndrome. The reason why Tri-somy 18 is less known is due to the reality that seldom do the babies live past birth.

The defects were obvious, and they were severe. There were organs forming on the outside of her body that were supposed to be on the inside. Other bodily structures that are required to allow other parts of the body to operate properly were not forming as needed.

We were given a choice, to end the pregnancy soon, to free Amber's body from the turmoil. Or, carry the child until term, at which time the baby probably would not live more than a minute. In the weeklong window we had to decide, Amber was working in a flower bed at her parents' house, and the decision was made for us. On August 22nd, her water broke. We met at the hospital. It was a painful day. One of the most painful of my life. It was heart wrenching and traumatic to listen to the baby's heartbeat on the monitor until it slowed to an almost complete stop. Thankfully, a compassionate nurse finally cut it off. I know it was even more painful for Amber. Her pain was palpable. Not only in the giving birth to a still born daughter physically, but much more the emotional trauma was evident. Amber would never be the same. We would never be the same.

A friend of ours that I would shoot dope with helped his dad run a burial business. They donated a tiny little vault for our firstborn Miriam. Miriam Lane Renee. We spent a couple of days holding her lifeless body, grieving with her tiny little distorted body in the flesh. Eventually, it was time to let go. We kissed her and then placed her in the gifted vault and then in some of Amber's family's ground that had also been gifted in Draper, in an unmarked grave. The grave site is on a beautiful piece of rolling land down by the New River, surrounded by pasture. I only went back to that place a couple of times, and both shortly after her burial. I am told that one day, one of the family members made a grave marker for her. I am not sure what it says. I am ashamed to admit, I don't have the courage to go back out there just yet. I believe healing will be found through going there. I just have not yet. I plan to.

When Miriam died, a part of me died. A part of the part of me that died, is a part that I would prefer not to re-visit. In another sense, Miriam was my hope, and when she died and was buried, so too was my hope; dead and buried.

While recalling much of this story for the manuscript of this story, I stumbled upon old photos of Miriam, Amber, and I shortly after her death and before her burial. The photos reminded, she was beautiful. The pain remains.

In my mind, I believed that I had done all of things that I was supposed to do to be a good dad at the point that Miriam was stillborn. Obviously, there was plenty of evidence to the contrary, but like most addicts, I was delusional and self-deceptive.

Amber truly had done all the right things. And the payment received for trying to do right was a dead baby the size of my hand? Surely, I thought, there is no God, and if there is, I don't care too much for him or the way he operates this world with its jails, and lung cancer, and dope sickness, and dead babies.

Miriam

My understanding of how God operated and/or "blessed" humanity was still one that was based around the notion of weighted scales of good and bad. Therefore, efforts at "good" should tip the scales toward "good" things in life. The experience with Miriam not only challenged that theology once again, but it also ticked me off, because I believed it to be true, as that was the only understanding of God's action that had been formed in me (to no real fault of anyone).

I kept taking the clinic's Methadone, making those daily ninety-minute round trips, but when I got back to Pulaski, it was crack-cocaine time. That is how I tried to cope with the loss of a child. By smoking crack. Not the best coping mechanism. It's important to note that the Methadone functions only to block the euphoria caused by opioids. Most other substances can still be used and abused, and the cravings for those substances are still very active for one in active addiction.

Through daily crack smoking, my previously delayed downward spiral recommenced and I was once again "off to the races" and unfortunately, Amber was in tow. It was she who cracked first and fell off the wagon. I totally understand how, given her grief as a mother. Had she had not fallen off first, it would have only been a matter of days before I fell and drug her down with me, leading the way toward the dark, disease-ridden abyss of degradation, dereliction, and death.

Bad checks were written, stolen from different parents check books, more jobs were procured and then lost. Losing jobs was "old hat." Taking checks without permission and committing forgery were new lows that I never imagined ever reaching. Addiction has a way of permitting the addict to achieve things they never desired to achieve in ways that are far from illustrious. Most of what I achieved during this shameful and painful period of life was mass destruction, deceit, and many other manners of harm.

A large amount of our "coping" time was spent finding cemeteries or other places sparsely occupied by the living so we could hit the pipe, or if no pipe was available, the pop-can. The pop-can bowl is a piece of junkie ingenuity that involves poking some holes in the can in proper places, and some cigarette ash covering the holes to prevent the rock from melting into the aluminum. The days of woos were long gone by this point. We were straight crack smoking. Proper crackhead use only.

I had hit a new bottom, but since the Methadone kept me from using pain pills, at least I was not shooting up; a justification I would offer myself.

Strange thing about addicts and bottoms, we have a knack for finding lower ones, and always with a justification in tow.

Previously, Amber and I had been living together in her basement apartment at her parent's house, she had quit going to college around the time she got pregnant with Miriam, but the basement apartment remained. As the crack smoking continued, I was kicked out of there. I was too ashamed to crawl back to either parent if they would've even had me. I suggested to my Maw-Maw Fisher that I might need to come and live with her and Paw-Paw. When my mom caught wind of that plan, it was no longer a viable option.

Seemingly out of options, I would hang out in the alleyway behind Amber's folks' place in town, while Amber spent time inside her parents' home, taking showers, eating, and doing whatever else was needed to fulfill the family obligations to make it seem that she was leading a normal sort of life. Once she was done, she would drive one street over to pick me up out of the alley. We would run the roads and find places to smoke until we exhausted every option for the day. I would then be dropped off at the Budget Inn motel, where I could get a small room for $29 a night. This rhythm continued until I no longer had $29 left one night, and Amber snuck me in prior to asking and then convinced her parents to let me come back as I waited quietly in the basement.

During this time of trying to stay numb, I had a counselor at the Methadone clinic who cared for me greatly. His name was Taylor. Taylor was a timid and kind man who was in recovery himself and who genuinely wanted to see me do good. The problem was I kept failing drug tests at the clinic and therefore, was not doing good. One day, Taylor had an idea, "What if we put you on a contract that states if you fail three drug tests you will have to leave the clinic? Would that be good motivation for you to stop using on the street?" I thought a moment, and in an effort to please Taylor, and to take another stab at being and doing good I responded, "Sure."

I signed the contract and was kicked out of the program about a month later, after being "medically detoxed" from ninety milligrams of liquid red goodness per day, down to zero, rapidly.

18

Roadrunners

DURING THE TIME BEFORE I got kicked out, there were a lot of road partners making the daily ride to the Methadone clinic from Pulaski or places along the way. Adam became one such carpooler for a season, Michael was too. Michael also happened to carpool with my Uncle J.W. sometime after I stopped making the journey.

The first two to ride with Amber and I were Terry and Bea. Terry was a scruffy looking fellow with a constant mischievous look on his face. Bea was small in stature, and as much as Terry projected mischievousness, Bea countered with kindness. She was mischievous, nonetheless. Both would take your money and run if they were in a tight spot, no matter how deep you perceived your friendship to be.

Bea gave birth to a baby girl that I adored, leading them to want to get at least some sort of clean. Social Services had been on Bea about the safety of the baby. She already had one child who was not in her care, so she longed to do good to keep her girl. The Methadone clinic was the answer that Terry and Bea needed, or so it seemed. It was Terry and Bea who taught us that if you eat ice cream after taking your dose, it would cause it to kick in quicker (no scientific evidence exists that I am aware of to support the claim). We stopped by the McDonald's near the interstate every day on the way home, as did most others we knew from the clinic, hoping that the little boost of frozen dairy sitting on top and within a paper-wrapped cone would give our incoming clinical high a little boost of its own.

I had started to run with Terry a good bit outside of the clinic rides. He was as slick as a greased-up possum. When he would go to court (which was often), he would throw cigarettes in the elevators that he knew from experience the inmates would be transported on. The cigarettes tossed would mostly likely have been stolen by Terry from the gas station in Grahams Forge that we stopped at regularly on the way home from the clinic. In the middle of the store, with snacks on both sides, a large, unlocked, glass case full of cigarette cartons was an easy target for someone of Terry's level of thievery.

Terry was also the one who was holding his neck screaming in make believe pain, when on the way to the clinic, a man pulled out in front of us, forcing me to swerve and end up in a median in front of *Shoney's*. The poor old fool gave Terry $80 and left the scene of the accident. All I was worried about was switching seats with Amber due to the fact that I was once again driving without a license. We received no money, only a wrecked up front-end of a car.

Terry was also famous in our circles for his insurance scams. They went like this: Person A has a car with full coverage insurance on it. Terry would work with Person A to crash the car in a predetermined way that they hoped they would not get hurt in. Often, this would involve a collision with a tree. When the rescue squad came, Terry would be "injured." That "injury" would lead him to sue Person A's insurance company. Upon settlement, Terry would pay Person A their agreed upon portion of the settlement.

It was wild ideas like that which should have taught me better than to go riding with Terry and Bea and another man on a hot summer day. The other man had told Terry that he had a check that he needed a ride to the bank to get cashed. I was the only one with access to transportation, so I got the call. I was going to make $100 for my services and we were going to get high. In Amber's new to her white Mercury, I picked up Terry and Bea and the three of us headed to some apartments across from KFC, where we picked up the man. The man told me which bank to go to, and we entered through the drive thru. The kind lady on the other side of the glass opened the door, and having pulled up into the drive thru so that the bank door would be even with the four-door car's back door, I made it so the man could put his own check into the container for transport inside.

Quickly, the woman placed the check back into the container and sent it back to the man in the backseat, informing him that they would not be cashing a check that was made out to his sister. He argued for a minute, and then we drove on, per his direction, to another bank. At the next bank, there was a similar outcome, but with lots of strange looks from the tellers inside. I began to sense there was more to this than the check being made out to his sister. When the check made it back in the car this time, I asked to see it. Indeed, it was a check made out to his sister. And, to make things more embarrassing and illegal, the check was from one of the short-term loan agencies that send checks in the mail with a contract included on the back of the check. A common wording that can be found on the front of all these checks is "FOR DEPOSIT ONLY."

I was irate. I told the man I was taking him back home (to his sisters) and I told Terry and Bea I was not happy with them either for linking me up with this knucklehead, who actually thought he could cash in a loan made out to his sister from a company that put "FOR DEPOSIT ONLY" on the check.

After we dropped Albert Einstein off, we headed back toward the one room apartment that Terry and Bea were living in. About halfway there, blue lights appeared in my mirrors, sirens were blaring. I pulled into a former 7-11 convenience story that had been sold and renamed, Guida's Market. For some reason, the number of blue lights that I was seeing began to multiply. The number of flashing lights and blaring sirens reminded me of the annual fire parade.

The intimidating, tall, moustache-wearing cop, who had recently turned in his undercover status (everyone knew him by then) to acquire rank of some sort in uniform, approached me on the driver's side. Under my seat was a pill crusher (the type that anyone can buy at any pharmacy) that had been filled with Xanax in the compartment within the crusher lid. When I first saw blue lights, I threw the emptied crusher under the seat after eating the handful of Xanax.

The former undercover policeman advised me to get out of the car, while two other officers advised Terry and Bea to do the same. Terry and I were searched there in front of Guida's. Bea had to wait until a female officer arrived to do the same. The female officer took Bea inside to the bathroom for her search, for some reason I can't remember. I do remember the big, intimidating, ranked officer, asking me if I would grant him permission to search the car. When I inquired as to why they desired to search my car, I was told it was over someone trying to pass a bad check. I told the officer that he was not going to find a bad check or any check in my car, and the check he was looking for was thrown out of a car window on Memorial Drive by the man he really should be talking to.

There was no doubt he knew who he should be talking to, and he knew there was probably no chance the check was still in the vehicle or in the possession of any of the three of us. Of course, with this opportunity he wanted to search the car, nevertheless. With the pill crusher under the seat, even though it was pill-less, there was no way I was letting him or any of them in that car without a warrant.

The Xanax really started to kick in after our searches and the initial conversation as to the check and its whereabouts. To say I was beginning to feel carefree would be an understatement. I still cared enough not to let the car be searched, but other than that, I was feeling quite euphoric and strangely (and I'm sure to the police, aggravatingly) confident.

"I'll call the judge and get a warrant," said the former undercover narcotics agent.

"Call him or her. I don't care."

He pulls out a phone, dials a number. Hangs up.

"Nobody picked up. We will wait and try again in a minute. Or you can just let me search the car."

"We will wait."

Five minutes later, he pulls out the phone, dials a number. Hangs up.

"Still can't get the judge?" I asked.

"Not yet. I'm going to keep trying if it takes all night."

The summer heat was really bearing down on us all at this point. Sweat beads had begun to form on the heads of all of Pulaski's finest. I'm sure there were beads rolling down my skull as well, but if they were, I couldn't feel them. Terry loved stuff like this, especially when he knew he stood no chance for being charged for anything. He was laughing and having a good time talking with and taunting the police officers. Bea was aggravated at Terry enjoying himself so much, and for being cuffed and seated out in front of a convenience store in the heat.

The officer pulled out the phone once more, looked at me and said, "It sure is getting hot out here. It would make things go so much quicker if you just let us in the car."

"Nah, man, I'm good. You ain't lying, it is hot though."

He dials a number, and shortly thereafter, hung up. Who knew who he really tried to call. Maybe it was a judge. Maybe not. A dear friend of mine, who for this story shall remain nameless, used to call the time and temperature number, or the library's story time number, and pretend to have lengthy conversations with "a dealer" when he was fixing to take someone's money for some dope and not come back. I knew something similar was possible for a seasoned narcotics agent desperately trying to search the car of known users.

"Alright, since I did not get the judge on the phone to issue a warrant, you are free to go. I would not hang around with "Deposit Check Only Boy" if I were you. And I would stay away from those two too," he said as he pointed to Terry and Bea. The three of us got into the car and left. I don't remember how I got home, wherever home was for that night, I just know that I drove.

I hold no ill will toward the police for any encounter I ever had with them. There were some uniformed folks who treated me with dignity and compassion. I do find it frustrating that such great efforts were taken in those days in my hometown to send people to the regional jail for things that were not that serious. When the opioid epidemic began in our part of Appalachia, our police force locked in, in a very strong-armed way. There was no grace and no tolerance in most cases.

For the sake of so many I have known, I wish rehabilitation would have been prioritized over incarceration. It simply wasn't. I'm not sure how it could have worked, I just wished it had a chance to. To be fair, the emphasis needed for treatment and rehabilitation was not the responsibility of the police department or the sheriff's office. The priority of incarceration over rehabilitation is, and was, a systemic issue, requiring the change at levels above the boots on the ground.

Had that pill crusher been found at that point of my life, with only residue in it, that could have been enough to send me away, and it most likely would have. To be clear, my actions were my own, and there were laws in place that I knew needed to be abided by, and yet I chose to break those laws. To be sure, I was not alone in making such decisions in those days, nor has then been a shortage of others making similar decisions since. What I am saying is that if the systems and institutions put the same amount of effort into rehabilitation that they put into prosecution that systemically (in large part due to privatization of the prison complex) leads to more recidivism, outcomes may have been and may be different for those who struggle with the disease of addiction and other matters of mental health that lead to incarceration.

There is no reason the United States should have the out of proportion number of the world's prison population that we do. I was taught in seminary, and it still holds true to this day, that although the U.S. has around

5% of the world's population, we have currently incarcerated a little over 20% of the world's prisoners. Make no mistake, addiction is the leading cause of whatever led to the incarceration for most of these inmates. To be sure, other places have addiction issues as well. It seems as if our ideas of "life, liberty, and justice" have become skewed by greed, in addition to laws manipulated by said greed, which diminish the personhood of some (as others have shown extensively, especially in regard to race and economic class), leading to the disproportionate number of incarcerations.

As for me, on many occasions, I found myself on the better side of the fine line that exists between incarceration and freedom.

After dodging the lockup that summer day long ago, I did stop running with Terry and Bea so much. Amber and I found that our life was changing during this time, and it would be best if we stopped hauling them around as much so that we would have the time necessary to tend to all the ever changingness. One day, later the year of the check incident, Terry rolled over in the bed to find Bea ice cold, dead at the age of twenty-eight.

Bea would not be the only of our Methadone clinic riders over the years who would pass away. A guy I worked with at Papa John's and his girlfriend, who I also worked with, became passengers on the white Mercury Methadone express at one point. We would meet at a place on the clinic route in between their West Virginia residence and our place in Pulaski. One day, a few months after his last ride with us, he nodded out and fell asleep at the wheel while driving in West Virginia, hit a tree, and died. He was in his mid-twenties

Mike and Ang were two people I was friendly with from the time of high school and the clinic days. They rode for a season. Later in life, at a young age, both overdosed. First Mike, then Ang. Like Bea, they left behind two children.

My buddy Nick was a longtime rider. A funny, good, kind guy who I worked with at a place making truck parts. Long after I left that job, and long after I left Pulaski, Nick was in the area around the clinic one morning. I cannot say for sure why. For whatever reason he was in that area, one day he drove his car into the path of a tractor trailer. He did not survive. There were four who would know him as their dad. Having been out of personal contact with Nick for years still did not lessen the impact his death had on my mind and my spirit. Death upends me, especially when it happens to the young. Later, I'll say more about what "upend" looked like at times.

Of all the people we gave rides to the clinic to, Donnie was probably the person who rode the longest. The period that Donnie and Nick rode with us together was the absolute best of the road running times to Galax. The two of them were like a backseat version of Abbott and Costello.

Donnie was not only funny, but witty, and he liked me as much as I liked him. We worked 3rd shift together at the company that employed my mom. That is until one night when Donnie ate too many Xanax and spent the whole shift passed out up against a wall. We were able to keep him hidden for most of the night, but the brute who was over the 3rd shift eventually spotted him seated, and propped up, in a back corner of our department, head leaned to one side, mouth agape. Donnie was supposed to ride to the clinic with us when he and I got off work. He would not be making it that day, as he had to take a trip with the 1st shift Supervisor of our department and the head of H.R. to the hospital for a blood drug test. I was headed out of work and into the parking lot when the company leaders were bringing Donnie out of the building and heading toward the company van.

"Where. . .are. . . .we. . . .goingggggggg?" Donnie, who at this point was looking much akin to Droopy the Dog, asked.

"To the hospital for a blood test" one of them replied.

"*Whyyyyyyyy*?"

"Because we think you're high."

"*Wellllllll. Fuckkkkkk* it. Let's *nn-gooooooo thennnnnn.*"

I loved me some Donnie. Unlike Terry and some others, he was a good friend through both thick and thin the years we hung out. By this point, you've probably guessed it, Donnie left this earth too soon, aged forty-eight, leaving behind a sweet and loving wife, and three great children. His aunt told me it was an overdose. He was such a good dude. Heartbreaking.

There were others from our clinic trips who died as well. Sadly, there are probably some who have died who I have forgotten. That holds true for non-clinic folks from around our area who I have known as well. I suppose it becomes easy to forget some when there are so many. I did not go to my graduating class's twenty-year high school class reunion. I saw on social media that they had turned a table into a candlelit memorial for nearly thirty some classmates who had died. I made my own list of the ones I knew were a part of our class who were also dead. The number was over forty, not quite fifty (at that point).

19

Gabriella

Prior to being removed from the Methadone clinic, I managed to land a decent enough job in Dublin, which through a series of events and reference check conversation with a former boss, led to an even better job at a log home manufacturer one county over in a little village called Elliston. Through a strong relationship with that former boss-turned-boss again, and his successor, I was able to maintain my employment at this place way longer than I had any other job, and way longer than I should. I look back on those years, and that job, and I see grace abundant, as any good Wesleyan should. These two supervisors were once again examples of people who believed in me when I did not have the ability (nor the willingness) to believe in myself.

Considering my previous employments, I needed all the job-related grace I could get. To illustrate this point, here is a list of jobs and reasons for termination pre-log home employment: Pulaski Furniture Company – left for Dish Network, Dish Network – fired for excessive absences – Bond Cote (mom's employer) – excessive absences, Ethan Allen (in former PFC building I worked in previously) – excessive absences, Dish Network again – excessive absences, Papa John's – alleged embezzlement, Southwest Times – excessive absences, Bond Cote again – excessive absences, TMD Friction (brake manufacturer) – you can probably guess, Walmart (Tire and Auto Center) – failed drug test and escorted out during training on day 1. Hilariously, I still receive opportunities to join class action lawsuits against them that pay according to the length of your employment. Findlay Industries (making interior truck parts for Volvo and Mack trucks) – left for log home company job in Elliston, where I for many months remained one absence away from termination. Career advancement was never my goal in these years; just the paycheck, and then the next one if there were to be a next one.

After getting the boot from the clinic, I wasn't sure how I was going to keep the log home job I loved without the Methadone. To be honest, I wasn't sure how I was going to stay alive (or consistently high) without the Methadone. During this time, more and more of my acquaintances were dying from overdoses. Ironically, and sadly, the majority were overdosing from a combination of Methadone and benzo's (i.e. Xanax). In fact, most of the overdoses of friends and acquaintances that I know of happened because of this mixture, in which one half of the mixture is supposed to be the cure for their opioid addiction. Also, anyone who has ever had to come off Methadone will tell you, the dope sickness experienced is far greater than the dope sickness from other opioids.

In a strange twist of good fate, after exiting the clinic life, Amber and I had moved into the single-wide house my mom and I bought in Draper. My great-aunt had been living there in the years since the lack of electricity forced my departure. In the Spring of 2003, when we found out Amber was pregnant again, my mom agreed to negotiate my great-aunt's departure from the trailer so we could have a home for our soon to be family of three, while in no way assuming that all would go well with the pregnancy. Our previous experience did away with any such assumptions.

We went to all our "high-risk" neonatal visits and things were looking good. And we found out, we were having another girl! A healthy one!

Gabriella Jordan McKay Largen blessed us with her presence December 3rd, 2003. All of us were ecstatic. I longed to be a good father to this beautiful little girl. I did not get off to a good start on the good father thing to say the least. When Amber was in the operating room for the C-section, I was supposed to be in a locker room changing into some scrubs so that I could be in a hallway viewing area once Ella arrived. Due to Amber requiring anesthesia I was not allowed in the OR. Shortly before they took Amber in, a friend had delivered a little celebratory cocaine to me. I got so caught up snorting it, I never made it to the delivery room hallway. It wasn't until a nurse opened the locker room door and yelled at me that my daughter was here that I realized how long I had been in there. This was and is one of the most shameful moments of my life. I was so far caught in the grip of addiction that not even the high of the birth of a beautiful baby girl was enough for the day. Perhaps it would have been, had I waited to get high long enough for her birth to take place. Nobody but me ever knew this sad fact, until I wrote these lines.

Daughter, forgive me, I know not what I do.

With that said, one of the most vivid memories of my life was after I came out of the locker room and joined the nurse. After beholding my baby girl, we wheeled Ella down the main hallway and toward the hospital nursery. In the hallway, just outside of the nursery entrance were Amber's parents, my mom, and my dad. All were smiling like donkeys eating briars. I was hopping up and down, while pointing down toward the plastic crib. While Amber was in the OR recovery room coming to, we were all in the hallway celebrating new life together, overjoyed, like we collectively (and perhaps individually) had never been before. There were hugs and high-fives all around. The coke soon wore off, and I didn't mind.

20

Methamphetamine

ELLA WAS GOING TO be a big part of my saving grace; eventually. First, I had to self-destruct some more. In the meantime, she was healthy and that was all that mattered. Never had I been in presence of a more beautiful creature. As to be expected, despite my intentions to be dad of the year, narcotics continued to dominate my life, this time in a new fashion.

Amber was getting "take home" medication from the clinic, because unlike me, she could pass a drug test. She was doing quite well and did not mind sharing her meds with me to keep me from being dope sick, to keep me slightly high, and to keep me at work earning an income. An alternative solution to keep dope sickness away emerged, even though I was not dope sick. It was just the thought of one day becoming sick that terrified me to the point of something new.

One of my original childhood friends had been delving into the world of crystal methamphetamine for quite a while. It had never intrigued me much. Mainly because of what I saw it doing to my old friend. He would go on a good long crystal run and then reemerge looking as if he had been doing battle with the devil himself. Being up for days on end, and picking my skin to the point of woundedness, did not appeal to me the same way that shooting Oxy's and nodding out and drooling on myself did. Nevertheless, the two of us started consistently running together again and I acquired a taste for the stuff. The downer effect of the take homes I was sharing with Amber, and the upper effect of the methamphetamine balanced one another and made me feel just high and productive enough.

Using the crystal meth was easy and the methods were plenty. There was the old-fashioned way of snorting it, once the glass like substance had been crushed into as fine of a powder as possible. It burned like the devil going up, but depending on the quality of the dope, it had an decent taste as it worked down. Then, there was the smoking option. Some users had meth pipes, others used broken light bulbs, and then there was the popular option for most, including myself in those days, aluminum foil smoking boats. For the really brave (and especially dumb), there was also the option of shooting up the methamphetamine. I used crystal in that fashion a few times but found it too intense for my liking. (All references for how all these methods can be used in a detailed way have been removed from this copy to eliminate the possibility of this work being utilized as a teaching method. The same holds true for the other forms of drugs and their detailed manners of usage as well).

Upon moving back to Draper, I discovered that all my old running mates from the earlier Draper days (who remained) had fallen in love with crystal meth as well, including my good buddy and next-door neighbor Rocky. Rocky's nickname was Bones. He was so skinny he made Barney Fife look like the Hulk. Rocky needed the crystal's increased effect of high metabolism as much as a chicken needs two beaks. Speaking of beaks, Rocky had a big bushy mustache under a thin and pointy nose. He always wore a hat, and most of the time a wry smile as well. Rocky was a good man and a good neighbor. He loved beer, just as he did riding his Harley Davidson Sportster, and he also loved to do a line or two of meth or coke, but he knew when to stop.

Rocky always managed to hold down a good job working in the landfill despite his partying. He was responsible for covering up the stuff that was dumped in the landfill through operating a large piece of machinery. He called himself a "Sanitation Engineer." Rocky was one of the few who could function and still go hard. I envied him for that, and I learned a lot about functioning while going hard from him as a neighbor (at least until I couldn't function anymore). Sadly, a few years after I moved back to Draper, Rocky's functioning came to a halt when he shot himself in the woods he used to hunt following a failed relationship that had failed a few times before as well. I miss his boney self.

Long before that heartbreaking and unfortunate day, Rocky introduced me to a guy who was tied up with one of the more prominent biker gangs. He got quality crystal meth by the pound. This guy and me, we hit it off. I had an unlimited line of credit as someone who knew people who would buy the stuff up a little at a time until the pound was gone. A little

Methamphetamine

over a year after our beautiful and healthy Gabriella was born (the winter of late 2004, early 2005) I estimate that I did a street value worth of $10,000 of meth, while having my hands on at least twice that amount at some point.

One night, after being up for a few days, the by the pound biker gang dope man showed up at my door. A guy in Roanoke had taken his money and ran off in a weed deal. I think it was $750 at most, but it was enough that my man wanted to recoup what he had lost. The plan was: my guy's girlfriend was going to call the Roanoke guy from a different number and pretend as if she knew him. The bet was, the Roanoke guy would fall for it and come out of the apartment. At that time, my guy in the vehicle with his girlfriend would jump out to confront him, as his brother, their cousin, and I would jump out of our vehicle to assist in the confrontation by way of intimidation.

On the way up Interstate 81, my guy's brother, also well known to me, looks over to me and says, "There is a pistol under your seat. When we get there, you reach down there and grab it before you get out of the car." Only half believing him, I reached down under the passenger seat and moved my hand around, until I felt the unmistakable steel of the handgun beneath me. At this point, I didn't have much choice but to finish the ride. I also lost all ability to think straight. All I could think was "gun." This was not something I was comfortable with. Stuff like this was not and had never been "me."

We arrived at an apartment complex off Williamson Rd., the girlfriend made the call, and moments later, the young man came running down the steps, gleefully and eagerly to meet some attractive sounding female who he wasn't going to get to meet. We rushed out of the cars and confronted him just as he was about to open the door on his little sedan. Needless to say, he was shocked. If you have ever witnessed the genuine surprise of someone walking into a surprise party for themselves, his expression looked like that. However, he knew this was no party.

The poor guy pled with my guy to give him a chance to make things right. We each took turns assuring him that he was going to make things right. I, with a small, all black handgun stuck in the waist band of my pants. The negotiations took place for all of three minutes. He insisted he got pulled over and arrested and that is why he never came back with the weed that other night. The reason didn't matter, and finally the deal was reached. He would go back to his apartment and bring down $500 worth of crack to make things as right as they were going to be able to be made. He said that was all he could do, and I believed him, and my God how I hoped the man who mattered most in this situation believed him so I could get this gun off me and get back in the car and go back to Pulaski County where I belonged. We held his car keys and flip phone until he came back. He came back as promised, thankfully, peacefully.

From there, it was back down the interstate and back to my guy's apartment in Radford. He and the other four smoked all $500 up in about an hour. As the fumes and the smoke from the crack rock filled the place, I stayed to myself in a room adjacent from the others. It was one of the only times in my life that I remember turning dope down. At that point on that never-ending night, I had no desire. I needed some sleep. I needed to see my baby. I needed to get out of that smoke filled apartment and go home to Draper.

A new low. Still not low enough.

21

Undone

Almost immediately after I started dabbling in methamphetamine, Amber joined me. Ever since we first connected with one another after high school, we had been birds of a feather flocking together in a bird bath filled with harmful substances. I liked it best when she wasn't using for a few reasons, the main one being that I could get high for half the price, or half the work. Amber's crystal meth use would also bring an end to her Methadone take homes, which led to a total and complete end to her use of the "maintenance" medication, and therefore, the end of my use of it as well. Any "balance" I thought I had in life and using would be disappearing.

Ella was still taken care of during the early days of Amber joining me in crystal use. She was fed each day, loved on, had her diaper changed, and was never left alone. Thankfully, we had enough good sense still present in those early days to have others in the family care for her when we were really out of it. Such as the day we drove six miles down the interstate in the middle of the two lanes headed north, going anywhere between twenty-five to forty-five miles per hour. That nearly ill-fated day, I drove us off the interstate and parked at a gas station in Dublin. We woke up six hours later.

Like I said, we were doing okay, or at least we had convinced ourselves that we were doing okay. Obviously, we were far from okay, but there was still plenty of room for decline. "Okay" is a relative term after all. Most folk who fall asleep driving and then in a parking lot of a gas station near their home are typically not "okay" based off most standards of living.

As is almost always the case with addicts who live, things got worse. Things got worse in a way that I could never imagined. The unraveling of reality that Amber would go through paradoxically happened in a way best described as strangely, subtly, and suddenly.

It began with her adamantly talking of bugs infesting the home where I saw none. We "bug bombed" the house with the aerosol type devices almost weekly, leading us to find a place to stay until the toxicity had time to leave the trailer.

The spider bite I received during this time did not help matters. My forearm turned purple with the spider's poison that had been injected into my body by way of little fangs. Soon, in a folie à deux (the madness of two) moment, we were both convinced we had multiple spider bites. We eventually made it to the E.R. later that night and saw the physician who had cared for me as a child. He broke the difficult news I am sure the Pulaski E.R. medical team had lots of experience telling folks like us: there were no bites. Well, just the first one on my arm. The rest simply were not there, no matter how heartedly we tried to convince them that they were. We left the E.R. cussing and screaming.

Amber's paranoia continued to progress. Next it was the house was wired with listening devices, the government was out to kill her, and the only safe space for her to go to was (for some unknown reason) Australia. Before long, I was accused of operating a methamphetamine lab under the trailer with people living under the house tending it. If some object in the house were in a place that it had not been previously, she would be convinced and rather angered by the delusion that someone had snuck in and moved it just to mess with her. At one point, she went two entire paranoid weeks without any significant sleep. The longer the mind and body goes without sleep, the more intense the delusions become, until all that is left is delusion.

After participating in the few days long task of ripping out of the carpet from the entire house and throwing all the furniture in the yard to try and to appease some of her psychosis fueled concerns, and after having consulted Rocky and others to ensure she was having a mental breakdown and I was still mostly my usual self, I loaded Amber up with a handful of Valium so that she could sleep. My thinking was, if she sleeps, she will return to normal. In my experience of getting high, or having a bad trip when we were teenagers, was that you go to sleep, and you wake up better. Surely, the benzodiazepine aided sleep would work, and she would return to herself. As was often the case in those days, I thought wrong.

When she awoke from a good long slumber, it did not take long to realize she was not any better mentally. At that point, I feared for her and Ella's well-being when I was away at work. I investigated the options available to get her better, while knowing she was not willing to, nor mentally capable of agreeing to go anywhere for any sort of help. She truly was occupying a reality all her own. The only time I shared in her reality was in my hearing about her perceptions of it, that is, after I stopped sharing in the "reality" of her delusions as I did with the bug bites early on.

Amber's eyeballs were completely black. There was a haunting quality to her eyes. She looked as if she were someone from a movie that was possessed or bewitched. The more she began to embrace the reality she had come to occupy all her own, the more comfortable she was in it. Her paranoia gave way to a wandering of sorts. A wandering that led her from one end of the seventy-foot-long trailer to the other. At times it was as if she were gracefully gliding from end to end. When she bathed, she tickled and gently moved the water as I would imagine the Word of God doing at creation.

The gracefulness and gentleness and the nearly beautiful way she was becoming as the paranoid talking stopped, also quickly came to a stop when I found her in the garden tub, surrounded by candles, with water running out of tub and into the floor. She was not submerged, but it was apparent to me her plans were to soon be. The only option left on the table was to trick her to take a trip to town, where mental health professionals would be able to evaluate her and to petition a judge for a Temporary Detaining Order (TDO).

It did not take much time for those doing the evaluation of Amber's mental well-being to see that she needed help. The TDO was issued, and she was loaded up in the back of a police car and taken to the hospital psychiatric ward where I would one day get clean. Seeing her hauled off like that was as heartbreaking as losing Miriam or any of my friends or family. I wept uncontrollably. These are facts from that night and that period in our life that she still does not believe to this day. All she felt, and in many ways continues to feel, when calling back the haunted memory of those days, is betrayal. I felt and feel as if I had failed her. I had.

I still don't know if I have forgiven myself, not for the TDO, that had to happen; the regret I hold on to is for not protecting her better. Professionals in the field of psychiatry have often tried to console me, saying that the dope sped up something that would have most likely happened anyway.

For the selfish sake of my conscience, I hope they are right. There were signs early on which point to their being right, but who can say for sure? Either way, she didn't deserve it.

The psychiatric hospital they took her to first was in Radford, (an in-patient facility that had been moved to a larger hospital building from an old three-story brick structure that one of my heroes stayed in for a time). In Radford, it took a very short amount of time for their staff to determine they were not the place for her. They said her psychosis was too severe for what they had to offer.

From Radford, she was transported further down the I-81 corridor to Salem where she stayed for a full month until she was released, still very unwell. During that first month stay I visited a few times. I found that my presence did more harm than good for the both of us. As a firefighter later in life, and in ministry, I have witnessed scary things. What the medication Haldol did to Amber ranks at the top of the list of such things. It was on the first visit post-TDO that I witnessed the "Haldol Shuffle." For those who have watched shows with zombies such as *The Walking Dead* you can envision what the shuffle may look like. The legs move slowly as the body rocks in a haunting rhythm. Not only was the gait scary, but the appearance of her head and neck sent me into a pure panic. Amber's neck was cocked to one side. Her right ear, nearly touching her right shoulder. Her gaze went upward. Her mouth was opened so widely that it seemed impossible. To add to the terror and the sadness of it all, she made a noise that never stopped that sounded like a vacuum at a car wash. My bride was the walking dead.

I pled with the social worker there to fix whatever caused her to walk and look like that. The response I received was, they did not believe that what she was projecting in that moment was her actual experience. In other words, they said it was all an act. That "diagnosis/explanation" was a load of bullshit. The Haldol treatment soon ended, but she was not getting significantly better with the next attempted regimen, but at least the shuffle ended. With that said, as is the norm in the U.S., after so many days, in this case twenty-eight, the insurance company (not the hospital) said that she was better, and it was time for her to come home.

Upon getting out of the hospital prematurely, Amber came back to the carpet-less and nearly furniture-less Draper trailer. I had been up for a couple of days when she came home. I crashed out on the couch through no choice of my will. I awoke to find my bride sitting on the bare particle board floor, legs crossed crisscross-applesauce, steak knife in her lap, staring at me almost like a mother watching her child sleep. Knowing I was not forgiven for the TDO and the month-long mental hospital stay, and knowing she was still quite unwell, I got out of the house as fast as I could, called my mom and her mom who came over and had her recommitted. This time, with the hospital staff fully aware she was not well enough to go home, they were prepared to receive her and to continue the trajectory of care that had already begun prior to the premature discharge.

After this stint in the hospital, Amber got mostly well. It would not take as long of a hospital stay this time for her to get out, well enough and as well as she was going to be for a while, they said. Her parents made the wise decision of convincing her to come and live with them. I still had Ella in my care and was doing the best I could to care for all her needs. One day, I received a call from Amber wanting to see Ella. I was terrified of allowing such a visit to happen without me, due to the way Amber had been looking and acting the last several times I had laid eyes on her. Yet, they were mother and daughter and I could not live with myself had I withheld contact between the two of them.

I met Amber and her mother in the Pulaski Wendy's parking lot for the handing over of Ella and her car seat for a visit. It would be over a month before I saw my child again. In the Commonwealth of Virginia, when it comes to custody of children, if there are no legal documents, possession of the child is equal to full custody so long as you are one of the parents. They set me up and got me. There never was an intention for a "visit." It was always about gaining possession. Having the visitation at her parents' house, there was no doubt I was not going to stick around for it. Then, I was bitter for how it went down. Now, I am not. She was safer there.

I never put Ella directly in harm's way like some of the folks do in the stories you hear or read in the news where people leave their kids in locked cars or at home for days with no food or water. That was not the case. Even at my lowest points, and even at Amber and my collective lowest point. Ella's well-being was always a priority. But as for myself, aside from the time I was cuddling Ella or asleep, I was constantly in harm's way and my priority was certainly not my well-being. My main source of harm was myself.

Aside from my main source of harm being myself, there was also the paranoid delusion within me that maybe Amber was right and there were some, mysterious and unknown others, out to do us harm. One night, in the trailer by myself, I noticed around daybreak that someone had pulled into the top of my driveway and then backed immediately out of it. I was so afraid, I darted from one end of the house to the other. My thinking was, if they start shooting through the walls it may be harder to hit a moving target. The next morning, the same thing happened. This time, I wisely just hit the floor and waited for the daylight that was fast approaching.

The morning after, day three, I was still awake. Outside, it was that pitch black kind of dark, that darkest of darkness that always precedes the rising light of morning. I had resolved that if the people who were harassing me were going to keep it up, I had to respond. Plus, at this point, I thought their intention may have been to steal my dog. Wanting to shoot up my house was one thing, the potential that they were out to steal my dog was taking things too far.

I had a wooden, *Louisville Slugger* baseball bat by the door (I had grabbed it and got into a good batting stance by the door when Rocky came over unannounced just a day or two before). Out of nowhere, headlights appeared in the driveway once more, piercing through that darkest of darks. I sprang up, grabbed the bat, headed out the back door, down the deck steps, onto and up the driveway I went. Bat raised high, I watched taillights go down the road.

I looked down in the driveway and saw the three most recent copies of the Roanoke newspaper I had recently subscribed to.

Toward the end of the month that I was without Ella, and she and Amber had gone to live at Amber's parents' house, I was still by myself in the Draper trailer. When that first month without my family came to an end, I now dwelt with no electricity, no food, no hope. I had not been to work in weeks. I laid claim to FMLA early at one point during Amber's initial hospitalization. The trailer's floors were now part vinyl and part bare boards due to the carpet ripping and the incompletion of the reflooring project that started and had yet to be completed as such methamphetamine fueled projects tend to do.

One night, trying to fall asleep on a mostly deflated air mattress by candlelight, I began crying as I had never cried before. This was a new bottom, the depths of which I was unfamiliar. It was yet, another new low point in life. All the years of trying to find my identity and get to some place I was supposed to go in life had landed me here, on the floor. I was not an outlaw hero. I was a broken boy who was supposed to be a man. "Finally at your full potential," I thought to myself. I wanted my girls back, and I wanted to get better, and to do better, and to be better. The problem was, I was too far in the grip. The void had almost consumed me completely. Like my hope, barely any light remained.

Things had progressed so quickly. What had always been serious, but still managed to feel like play, now only felt serious beyond the point of despair. The indictment and probation, the loss of Miriam, the trip to rehab, nothing had ever made me feel as low as I was feeling in the wake of Ella not being under the same roof. "To hell with crystal meth" I thought, "I never even liked it in the first place." Believe it or not, I wasn't lying. That night I also thought, "The damage is done. And what is done, cannot be undone. I am undone. I am done."

22

Reuniting's

MY DAD HAD BEEN a part of my life just as much as the rest of my family throughout my years of drug abuse an adult. In other words, he didn't see me much, but he certainly had not given up on me. Out of a great love for me, after the Draper house was no longer fit for occupancy in its state at the time, dad took me back into my childhood home on Largen Hill Ct. He helped me get straight enough to come off FMLA and keep my job at least. Even better, in just a couple weeks' time on the hill, I was able to have enough stability to have Amber and Ella back as well. We shared the bedroom that was my bedroom as a boy, and I was grateful. We didn't have a bed frame, but at least we had an actual mattress that did not require air. Ella had the love and support of both of her parents, all her grandparents, and my Maw-Maw Largen, her great-grandmother next door. We all had some structure and stability. Life was getting better, and I felt more responsible as a twenty-three-year old husband and father.

As good and familiar as being back with dad and my family in the home I grew up in was, I found something else that felt good and familiar that I had been estranged from for a couple years at this point: the needle and Oxycontin. I never really got "clean" in the transition from the needle and Oxycontin to the Methadone, to the crack, to the crystal meth, and back to the needle and the Oxycontin. There were moments of brief relief, but it was a constant trading of this thing for the other. There, back at dads, with my family, I settled back into the routine of using the one substance I enjoyed the most; the one that offered the sweetest escape, by way of the harshest means. I daily questioned why I allowed myself to stop shooting up and to use anything else in the first place. All it took was an after work, drop in visit to Hogg's best friend Poochie's apartment, and one shot, for Oxycontin to win me back. I did not play hard to get.

Not having to pay rent or utilities or grocery bills freed me up to use my entire paycheck to buy pills. Of course, the paycheck alone wasn't enough, so I had to hustle here and there to make it from one week to another. Hustling usually involved making $5 or $10 here or there as a middleman, or in some cases as the middle man of the middle man. Like a good addict, I found ways to get high by any means necessary. The worst thing that ever happened is when the log home company started paying us bi-weekly as opposed to weekly; I really had to hustle then.

Amber stayed clean the majority of the time during this season of life as she readjusted to life and her medication. I was not only proud of her, but I was happy for her. I was also happy that I only had to find the ways and means to get one of us high on OC's.

It was in this stretch of time in which I started back shooting OC's that Hogg died. A few years before I came to know Hogg, he had been shooting dope and went a little too far. He passed out with the needle in his arm, halfway through a shot. This meant, he had worked up the shot, inserted it into his vein, pulled back the plunger, filled the syringe with a mixture of his blood and the dope prior to passing out. He awoke, a good while later, not knowing that it had been a considerable amount of time since the mixed blood had been in the syringe, he thought it had been seconds, a minute at most. He hit the plunger and sent the mixture into his bloodstream.

Endocarditis is the medical term for the condition that he had because of reintroducing the old blood back into his blood stream; the damage it did to his heart was irreversible. Stuff like this often happens to addicts who shoot dope because finding a vein that is not already collapsed from overuse is hard to do after so much time and so many shots. Veins just don't hold up after a certain point. Once a good one is found, most people want to keep it open for as long as possible, either consciously or unconsciously.

I believe that because of the condition he had, Hogg knew that he was going to die young, and so he went as hard as he could to bring it about as quickly as he could. Sadly, for those of us who liked and loved him, it didn't take too long for his end to come.

The day of Hogg's funeral I went to pick Poochie up after he received permission from his probation officer to have a two-hour reprieve from his house arrest so that he could mourn the loss of his oldest friend. It was

Hogg that introduced me to Poochie, and I was glad that he did on many levels. He too was a good friend.

Pooch's house arrest was brought about by a drug charge. His lawyer had argued that his health, and the health of his mother was so bad that they needed each other to be well. It was granted. I was extremely grateful that in addition to the house arrest be granted, his reprieve from it long enough to go to his best friend's funeral was allowed. Even if it later turned out that it would not have been much different if we both stayed home.

Poochie and I shot up a lot of dope before heading out to the funeral home. That day we were fortunate enough to get our hands on some Dilaudid; in those days of opioid use in Pulaski County, this would be the equivalent of opening a pack of baseball cards and finding a Mickey Mantle rookie. This prescription painkiller was a rare find in the years of Oxycontin saturation. Dilaudid is a distinctly different high than that of an Oxy when shot up, in a good way for the junkie. Poochie and I were obliterated.

I don't remember getting to the funeral home, but I do remember Poochie and I criticizing some of the pallbearer choices Hogg's mother had made. "Greg up there raising hell, seeing who she got carrying his big ass into the ground" Pooch remarked. "He hated half their asses." I said. We both fell asleep during the funeral, each with his head resting on the other for the duration of the thing, until it was time to go and watch them put our friend in the ground. The next week, I went to the barbershop; it was my barber's dad who officiated the funeral. My barber said, "My dad said he really let that crowd at Hogg's funeral have it. Told them what they needed to hear but didn't want to hear. Yes sir, he let them have it." I smirked a little, not letting him know I was there (at least in body) and said, "Good for him. They need to hear it."

Following the winter of the crystal meth binge, until the summer of 2005, I shot a lot of Oxycontin into my arm. So much so, as an aging man many years after, I can still see the scar tissue with perfect clarity. To this day, you should see some of the lab workers reactions at the doctor's office, when they tie me off and start pressing around my arm, and if I see they are struggling, I say, "Trust me, just put it there" as I point to the tiny scar.

I shot a lot of dope at Poochie and his mother's apartment during this stretch of time. He and I loved hanging out and talking about sports when we were conscious enough to talk. Poochie was a good athlete before dope, and some other sicknesses, started to get the best of his physical ability. Pooch and some other guys had a good softball team around the time that my dad and the Lee Riders were playing two nights a week at Loving Field. Poochie could tell me every time that his team won, and who was the drunkest or most messed up when it happened.

One thing I admired about Pooch and his mom was the way they cared for the incarcerated. They were always looking after an inmate or two by putting money on their jailhouse commissary books and sending them cards. Now, to be clear, these cards are not what you are probably expecting when I say "cards." A card coming from their apartment postal box was a special card that had been worked on greatly.

Here's the deal: a common greeting card would be purchased. An OC would be worked in a syringe. The mixed contents of the syringe would be squirted out onto the card. This process would continue until each part of the card was covered. When the card arrived at the regional jail, the CO's who sort the mail, would open it up, see that it is a card with nothing in it and thus, allow it to pass through to the inmate. Upon receiving their card, the inmate could eat on their card for however long they wished for it to last. Or, there was always the option of selling pieces of the card to other inmates for their commissary money. Addicts know how to adapt and to innovate, even to the point of utilizing Hallmark.

In terms of adapting, when it came to shooting up, the more seasoned junkie Jabe did not miss like the younger, amateur version. I became so good at working up pills and shooting them that I became able to work up a shot while driving a car and insert it without a miss. I may have only been going ten-miles-per-hour on an unoccupied two (or one) lane country road, but it was still quite the juggling act with a needle and a spoon. Another characteristic of most active addicts I've known (obviously myself included), they're impatient, especially if they have been dope sick, or even borderline.

Dope sick is not a fun sick. Not to say any sick is fun. It is just that dope sick is different. It is much like the flu, except you have the mental anguish of knowing there is something out there somewhere that can make you better, it is just that you do not have the means to get it, or the knowledge of where to obtain it. Body aches, chills, headaches, an overall restlessness of the body, the inability to sleep, the constant thoughts of schemes or solutions that could make the sick go away, and of course the nausea and other not so pleasant side effect that involves many trips to the bathroom. Like I said, not fun.

To be clear, I seldom found myself sick. I had the ability, like most, to find somehow or some way to knock the edge off until the financial situation, or whatever other situation was causing the lack of relief, was rectified. On days it was clear I was not going to get any opioids, I would buy a twenty-two or forty-ounce beer and a packet of Tylenol PM. I would eat the nighttime Tylenol and chug the beer as fast as I could and then wait impatiently for sleep. Sometimes, while living back on the hill, I could convince my dad to help aid my sleep through sharing some of his *Ambien*. Thanks for friends like Poochie, who knew what sick felt like, I never recall having to go to any bandage type of remedy two nights in a row.

23

Awakening

WITH MY DOPE SHOOTING ability elevated, and therefore no more abscesses to worry about, all I had to do this go around was keep my arm covered so the boss man or my parents could not see the nice little purple, spider bite looking, bruise around my constant site of injection. I managed to keep this up as best as I could, while working and being a family man (in my dad's house), as best as I could until one weekend in the summer of 2005.

It was one of those bi-weekly pay weeks and I had a good check. I, perhaps sensing the end of a good run, went to my main dope guy and handed him all the proceeds from two weeks of work. That Friday evening and Saturday, I, along with a good friend who lived with his mom in a Radford apartment, shot every last bit of that paycheck up; in between nod outs, we would play Mario Kart on an old Nintendo 64.

On Sunday, I returned home to the hill. Anytime in life I walked into the home of Sammy Largen, and he turned the television off, I knew something was up. On this day, he turned it off, and I noticed sitting there on the coffee table was a shoe box that I had stashed high up in my closet. The shoebox was full of used needles, many of which were dull or bent that I was nevertheless holding onto just in case the people at the Barn Feed Store wouldn't sell me anymore. A bent or dull set of works is better than no works at all. As for the feed store, I imagine you are wondering: to get a needle there all I had to do was tell them that I was giving my dog a shot. It was the same needle that you had to have a prescription for at the pharmacy if you took insulin.

My father opened the shoebox, questioned me about some rather high price baseball cards that were missing (he and my uncle J.W. were not only collectors but also active sellers of such) then asked why I always wore long sleeves, even in the summer. As if the fact that my walking weight was approximately forty lbs. light of my healthy weight, and the permanent racoon like circles under my eyes were not clues enough, he demanded I show him my arms. When I did, any hope he had that all his intuition may be wrong was cast out.

The run was up. I had burned all other bridges. He told me Amber and Ella could stay, but the only way I could was if I tried treatment again. In an act of what I viewed as temporary self-preservation, I agreed to treatment. This time, dad insisted it would not be the Methadone clinic. By then, the clinic's reputation had been tarnished, and in his eyes, mainly because of my own experience of staying high the whole time I was being "maintained" by the high-powered medication.

This time it had to be somewhere else. After calling my boss, who still somehow managed to believe in me, I checked into the local behavioral health hospital in Radford. Their specialty was dealing with varied types of mental illnesses. They also understood the correlation between addiction and such illnesses and offered drug detox and rehabilitation to some.

I cussed my father at intake, in another one of the most shameful moments of my life. He was there, again, offering me love and support as both of my parents had my entire life as best they could, and I repaid him with a vulgar tirade. I don't remember much after that. To be sure, the medicine they had in that joint worked to take the edge off.

I spent the week as an inpatient in a fog. I would watch television with folks who were parked in front of the tube in basically a vegetative state. I sat around and played cards with people as young as, or younger than myself who were all there for attempting to kill themselves or some other form of self-harm not related to drug abuse. The highlight of the day, each day I was there were the few times cigarette smoking was allowed on the patio. The whole experience reminded me a lot of my weekends in jail. We, rightly, were inmates who needed the structure of being told when they can eat, sleep, wash, smoke, and have recreation. We were not technically prisoners there, but most of us were prisoners of our own minds. How each of our internal incarcerations looked, differed a lot from inmate to inmate, but we were prisoners, nonetheless. History, my family's experience, and the mental health crisis has shown, some get paroled or freed from these mental maximum-security stays quicker than others. Recidivism remains high.

Awakening

After a week at the shiny newish St. Albans-Radford facility, I was released and committed to a few months of intensive outpatient care (IOP). This consisted of watching recorded VHS tapes of A&E's graphic addiction recovery show "Intervention." It is not clinically advisable, nor a recommended therapeutic practice to watch others shoot up dope on television while trying to stay clean. But that is what we did because that is what the little lady in charge felt best.

As a part of my discharge and the IOP program, I was also required to go to two, 12-step meetings per week (I chose Narcotics Anonymous, N.A.). I was to have a paper stamped and signed to prove attendance. I went to those meetings feeling great about life, due in large part to the new age opiate suppression medication my new doctor at the mental hospital had prescribed. It was less harsh than the Methadone, in that it allowed me to feel like me with only a slight euphoric feeling, while at the same time providing the same receptor blocking qualities that keep opioid cravings away.

While sitting in those first 12-step meetings, I encountered some people I knew, and some others I did not know. All our stories were similar. During meetings we would guzzle sweetened coffee out of Styrofoam cups and share our struggles, experience, strength, and hope. Before and after meetings, we would gather around the outer parts of the church parking lots we met in and chain smoke while talking about our day or life in general. Sooner rather than later, I didn't mind getting that paper stamped and signed. Sooner rather than later, I enjoyed being there and the miracle happened. My spirit began to awaken.

I stopped taking the new maintenance drug very quickly. In fact, I weened myself off it, motivated by the love and support I felt around me in the rooms of N.A. What the folks in N.A. didn't realize was, I was still hoarding all the pills I was supposed to be taking and selling them to folks like my childhood running mates, primarily Michael. To be honest, it took many years before I could say that our family was as financially stable as we were in the days that I went to meetings, stayed clean, and sold my medicine.

I saw this arrangement as a win-win. I was getting paid, and Michael and other old mates were staying off the deadly dope to boot, and at a lower price than they could anywhere else. Saintly work, I'd say. St. Jabe of Pulaski, from the Order of Buprenorphine.

Amber, Ella, and I were able to move out of dad's house and into our own rental home in just a few months. It was a 2-bedroom, one bath house in the town of Pulaski that was about 700 square feet in size, with a little concrete front porch, and a tiny wooden deck off of one side of the back. We rented from a Pentecostal preacher who paid $11,000 for it in 2001. Our rent was $450 per month, plus utilities. We loved it!

We had an eccentric neighbor named Pearl who told us as we were unloading the trucks and moving in that her dogs preferred to "shit in your yard" and that we should not be surprised if we saw flashlights in that same yard that her dogs pooped in on some rainy nights, because she and her family "dig for nightcrawlers out there so's we can go fishin'."

Life was good on Hickory Avenue for the young Largen clan, even if we were living in town. For once, my life had a mostly healthy rhythm. I did not miss shifts at work anymore. I had a good relationship with all my family. My daughter adored me, and I her. Amber and I convinced the landlord to let us have a cat. Before I knew it, Amber brought home a second cat that she "rescued" from a sawmill while on an insurance sales call with her mother. We were on our way. All that was lacking was a picket fence, which we could not put up so that Pearl's dogs could have a place to offload, and her family could have fishing bait. I had heard it said a time or two that you should love your neighbor as yourself. If we had to forego the fence to be neighborly, so be it. Anyway, if we had asked the Pentecostal preacher landlord if he would put one up, knowing him better now, I imagine he would have charged us $11,000 to do it.

24

Damascus

We started attending church with dad and Maw-Maw Largen right before we moved to the little Hickory Avenue house. We would rise early on Sunday, get Ella and ourselves ready, head down to the little white church by the creek on Alum Spring Rd. known as Jordan's Chapel. There we would be greeted by a lot of our family and others who I had known for years. The worshipping body there would sing a mix of old timey hymns and some older contemporary praise songs. The preacher would preach and then he would leave immediately to go to the next church he had to preach at. The church family would stay behind and share announcements and then dismiss for Sunday School or Hardee's. I chose Hardee's. Amber chose to teach a Youth Sunday School class and did so quite well I am told.

One Sunday, the pastor approached me prior to worship with a question I can promise, I never expected. He said, "I'm going to be out for a Sunday coming up, and it has been suggested that you serve as the speaker. Are you up for it?" To be clear, I had never done any sort of public speaking in my life. Neither the little bit of time I spent at community college nor in high school had I taken a class on speaking. When I did speak in the day to day, about 20% of the words were curse words (thankfully, as you can tell, I am down to way less than 1% now). And here this man is, who I barely know, asking me to stand behind a pulpit and say something. I told him I wasn't sure, and he said he would give me a few days to think about it. I had been clean for four months.

That week, after work one day, I came home and called the pastor with an answer of "yes." What did I have to lose? Maybe someone else could find hope in whatever I had to say (assuming I didn't cuss). I called him up with my affirmative response and he proceeded to ask me what scripture I would be using. "I have to use one of those?" I asked. He half-laughed and said, "Yes, you have to have one of those." I didn't read the Bible. Never had. I told him "I'll call you back."

I flipped through every devotional we had laying around the house until I found one that made mention of Isaiah 40:28–31. I felt it was perfect for me. *"He gives power to the faint, and strengthens the powerless. Even youths will faint and be weary, and the young will fall exhausted; but those who wait for the Lord shall renew their strength, they shall mount up with wings like eagles, they shall run and not be weary, they shall walk and not faint."* (NRSV)

I called the pastor up, proud as hell of my scripture, and awaited the day for my speaking. I still felt it was foolish for me to be asked to do such a task. Looking back, it was grace at work when I was asked. I suppose grace often looks and seems foolish at first encounter. But that morning, the last Sunday in November 2005, when I stood in that pulpit and looked out upon the pews, something felt different inside of me. I thought the different feeling was cool and all and I then proceeded to go on for a good ten minutes about stuff that I had no clue about. At the end of it, the congregation, many of which were blood kin, stood up and applauded. My ego liked the attention, but my spirit did not like the haunting possibility that I was supposed to be doing such things (and allowed to). After all, I sold my medicine, cussed, and smoked cigarettes.

The God whispers continued, especially as I took my spiritual life more seriously, thanks in most part to N.A. and in some part to the church. It was in 12-step recovery that I learned how to pray. My early prayers were carbon copies of the one we shared together in the rooms: *God, grant me the serenity to accept the things I cannot change, the courage to change the things I can, and the wisdom to know the difference.* Don't waste your time trying to find that one in scripture, it isn't there. Slowly, I began to find words of my own to communicate to this great and mysterious Other who I felt was certainly real, but seemingly distant.

One morning on my commute to the log home plant, I had my "road to Elliston" moment, which was much akin to what Paul experienced on his "road to Damascus." I was actively praying as I was approaching the Exit 118 exit ramp on I-81. To my right, a former satellite television call center that fired me twice. In my head, a voice spoke back as I prayed. A still, small voice. Not my own. I had for some months been praying to whatever and whoever was listening, on this morning as I prayed, I was told, "I am He. The God revealed to you through Jesus." I wept and celebrated the remaining fifteen minutes to work and then for some more minutes upon arrival. My spirit had awakened, with the help of the Spirit of God. This would prove to be a pivotal moment in life.

I shared my Damascus moment with Amber and the people in the N.A. rooms who I trusted the most. They were thrilled to hear that my spiritual awakening was deepening to a new level. Even the ones I told who were not Christian were ecstatic to hear that my prayer was responded to, and as a result, I was going to keep praying.

As I grew deeper in my faith, I grew more deeply grateful for life and my surviving it to that point. As I came to a better understanding of just who it was that I was praying to throughout each day, I felt increasingly compelled to pursue pastoral ministry. With that said, the more compelled I felt, the more I fought against said compulsion. After all, someone who is fresh off of jabbing needles in their arm should not make quick decisions, especially if it is a strange voice in their head telling them to do so.

I ran from what was certainly a call in my life for over a year. I preached one more time during that span of time. Otherwise, it was the new rhythm of life that played out each day, week, and month, and it was good. It was kind of like being on cruise control, except occasionally I would have to speed up or slow down to avoid any major disruption to the new and comfortable status quo. Then, 2007 happened.

February 13th, 2007 Revisited

THE DAY BEFORE VALENTINE'S Day was the night of my cousin Dina's funeral service. The family received visitors through a receiving line prior to the service. I remember hugging Priscilla, her mother, who remained seated on the front pew and saying, "I don't know what to say, but I love you." She responded, "You know what it is like to hurt. You know some of how this feels." Maybe there was some truth to what she said. Gazing across the front of the chapel, I was still overwhelmed with the thought, "That is supposed to be you."

I took my place behind much of our closest family, who took their place behind Dina's mom and dad. The preacher that night was from Draper, a former neighbor. I can't tell you a word Rev. Ernie said that night in Stevens Funeral Home's Chapel. I can tell you I remember the spirit with which he said it. And I can tell you, what had previously been a whisper from God up until that point, became an echoing shout of sorts; a shout reverberating off the chapel walls that only I could hear.

"That is supposed to be you." But the voice wasn't talking about in Dina's place as I would have imagined, or as I had previously believed. The voice was talking about Rev. Ernie. "That is supposed to be you. Up there. Comforting my people. In moments just like this."

25

Bethany

I LEFT THAT GRIEVING space with my family that night in February and headed back to Hickory Avenue. I told Amber what I experienced and told her I could not run from God's call in my life anymore. I told her and other family members and friends in the days that followed, that I would continue to put one foot in front of the other so long as God continued to open the right doors along the way. That was my promise to God, to them, and to myself.

Thanks to Mrs. Trivette's generosity, I had three college credits from my stint at the community college following high school. I knew more schooling would be required, but other than that, I had no clue what the process would entail for a guy like me to become a United Methodist pastor. I did what I was supposed to do, and I set up a meeting with my pastor at the time.

This pastor had always been helpful and supportive of me. He was and remains a good man. However, on the day of my appointment he was far from my biggest encourager. He told the truth. "People with backgrounds like yours definitely have a hard time making it in the United Methodist Church." Then he added, "For someone like you, considering where you have been, it is near impossible to be ordained." More hard to hear truth.

He continued, "It's easier to get licensed. Ordained, that's a whole another thing." The process for licensing can be complete in a year if all goes extraordinarily well. Ordination can take six-plus years (if things go well, and you already have most of your undergrad education). Not only is ordination more time consuming, but it is also more rigorous in terms of what is required of the candidate in terms of writing, education, and evidence of call.

That morning my pastor went on and on about the difficulty of living past my past and into a future of licensed ministry in the church, as well as pointing out the many years of schooling that is required for ordination and/or local pastor licensing. Heck, I thought I was just supposed to show up, tell him I was called to preach, and he would give me a Bible and a prayer and send me out. That didn't happen.

What had been a fire burning within me quickly turned into a flood of discouragement and hopelessness. The achiever in me finally spoke up within my conscience and through the tears as I turned up the hill on Hickory Avenue. As I parked, I shouted to God, "I will keep going so long as you keep making a way. Opening doors, cracking windows, whatever you do, I will keep going until I can go no more, but I will only stop because you have removed the way."

The next day, March 9th, 2007, I went to New River Community College and signed up for the next semester and a full-time load of night classes that allowed me to continue to work full-time and provide for our family. The wife of the pastor who married Amber and me was my admissions advisor. We had been married in somewhat a shotgun fashion, except her dad didn't show up. The shotgun was being held by Maw-Maw Largen. My best man was my old friend Matt. He gave me a handful of Xanax as a wedding gift, and I don't remember what all happened next.

Four years later, the preacher's wife was so excited to see someone who could barely stand up in his own wedding make such a dramatic turnaround. I was so excited to prove wrong anyone who didn't think I could do it. "Potential," I kept mumbling to myself.

My cellphone back in those days was a state-of-the-art flip phone. After leaving the community college, driving down Route 11, I called my biggest supporter, my Maw-Maw Fisher, and shared with her the exciting news of my calling into ministry and my enrollment in college. Not a religious woman herself, she was still over the moon excited and proud of me, if nothing else then for the education. She nor Paw-Paw Fisher had not even come close to completing high school.

After hanging up from my on-the-road conversation with Maw-Maw on March 9th, I made my way home to Hickory Avenue. Amber was excited for me that day. Together, we rejoiced. She was always a great student. Academic achievement is something she took seriously. She had since restarted her academic journey as well. That journey got paused in part because I came over to her basement one night with a pocket full of pills after playing softball at Loving Field. The two of us and Ella still lacked the picket fence, but at least we had goals, a good trajectory to get to those goals, and two cats.

Within the first thirty minutes of being home, my flip phone rang. On the other end was my other Maw-Maw, Maw-Maw Largen. In a tone of voice that I had not heard since that night my Paw-Paw Largen died, she said, "Jabey, I have some bad news now. Ok?" The world froze, my mind didn't race nor jump to any thought. "Adam was killed in an accident. Betty found out from someone from church who found out from his Granny. I'm sorry Jabey, but this is real."

I collapsed in total disbelief and in an excruciating grief. My body literally folded up within itself. We had lived across the road from one another for almost our entire lives. Our families were woven together as if they were one. We were supposed to grow old and play softball and do other stuff together for the rest of our lives, like going hunting and fishing. How could this be real? I sobbed uncontrollably. It felt as if my soul was emptying with each cry.

Soon after receiving the news, I called Adam's brother Kyle. Shortly after, I went up on their hill to visit. There we embraced and wept with one another as families do.

Adam and another guy had pulled their two trucks off the road. It was said originally that one truck had broken down and the other was coming to pull it. As Adam and the other fellow were bent down between the front bumper of one, and the back bumper of the other, an elderly woman crested the hill and came across the curve on this stretch of Belspring Road. She ran into the back of the one truck pushing it into the other and pinning my lifelong friend and the other fellow in-between the two pickups. I was told by someone at the scene that the other man died instantly, and Adam lived for a few moments. That same person at a N.A. meeting told me they prayed with Adam as his breath left his body, pinned there between steel and more steel. I thanked them.

Stevens Funeral Home's chapel, parlor and sidewalk were packed the night of the visitation with Adam's family. The line stretched all the way around the building. Cars lined the road in both directions. In all my life of visiting that chapel I had never witnessed a crowd like this. The grief was palpable among all of us there. The casket was closed. The casket was beautiful. Whitetail deer on each corner.

I bought two suits from a retail men's store in Christiansburg. One for the visitation and one for the funeral. I still wear them from time to time, a couple decades later. One is black with a little pinstripe. One is a medium shade of brown. Both have cuffed pants. Both were baptized with tears two days in March 2007.

The day after the visitation we gathered in the chapel for the funeral; the same chapel we gathered in the month before for Dina. Winky, Michael, Kyle, Adam's half-brother, his half-brother's brother, and I served as Pall Bearers. Jimbo Linkous from Largen Hill Court, longtime neighbor of my Aunt Betty and Uncle Elwood presided over the service. From what I remember he did a phenomenal job. I critique such jobs now, for myself and others. That day I just sat with a packed room of people, listening and hoping for a piece of peace. When the time came, the funeral home folks played Skynyrd's *Freebird* and we carried Adam and several floral arrangements out the back door.

The six of us given the honor, loaded him up in the hearse and made our way down the road. Not just "the road' but familiar roads, all the way until we got to Alum Spring Rd. The twisting two-lane country road that raised and formed us. The road that we got dropped off on by the school bus and raced each other up our respective hills from. The road that Boonie Breedlove and Paw-Paw sat across from one another from with frosted windshields as we waited to go to school. The road we were on when Winky punched me in the nose. Our road. Alum Spring Rd.

By a familiar little white church, we turned off that road, and up a little hill by way of a gravel path, to a field that sat at the top of a quarry that we played around and some of us climbed. We gathered in a familiar field. A field that we had trampled on for years. A familiar field we would carry him through. Standing by a freshly dug grave in the field stood a kind man who once gifted me a tiny burial vault. In this field, in that grave, the broken body of one of my very best friends in life was laid. Like Jesus one day in Bethany, this day in Pulaski, we wept.

26

Maw-Maw Fisher and Others

SHE WAS BORN IN 1939 and given the name Norma Lee Richardson. Her birthplace was in the countryside of rural Wythe County, right beside Pulaski County. The community that she was born into, was, and is, called Max Meadows. At some point early in life, she and her half-sister and three half-brothers were relocated to the town of Pulaski not too far from where her future husband John Fisher was raised.

There is a lot of Maw-Maw's Fisher's past that is shrouded, more so than any other grandparent. I have no doubts that her upbringing was rough. I am told she could be a bit rough as she aged as well. Earlier in life she was a daily drinker. Additionally, she chain-smoked Doral's. But I also knew that she loved me in a special sort of way.

Maw-Maw Fisher watched me as my parents worked for a good portion of my childhood. In the summer months when I was very young, each day there would be two fried, over easy eggs and buttered toast waiting on me when I came in the door. Lunch time could be any variety of things she concocted. During the school years that I got off the bus there at Newbern Rd. as opposed to Largen Hill Ct., I would be greeted with a turkey sandwich with mustard, and orange Kool-Aid. No matter the time of year, I could always count on orange Kool-Aid.

With only wood stoves and kerosene heaters for warmth, and box fans for cooling, the house was always at one extreme temperature or another. I was severely burned by one of the kerosene heaters when I was quite small and left unattended, while in Maw-Maw's care. I don't remember it happening, but I still bear the scar. I know Maw-Maw had to have felt awful.

Maw-Maw never drove a car and never had job. When we had to go somewhere, we walked. We walked a lot. To the convenience store at the bottom of the hill, to pay bills, to the grocery store, to visit family, and occasionally on special days to get lunch at the new KFC below her home. Wherever we walked, we were sure to return before 3:00. At 3:00, *Guiding Light* came on CBS, and it was never missed. If I didn't bother her while the soap opera was on, I could watch *The Flintstones* which came on at 4:00.

When I was a little boy and got out of line, she would break a switch from a tree and discipline me. When I got older and made mistakes aplenty, she would look at me chomping on a piece of gum, shake her head, and give me grace. Like Paw-Paw Largen, I spent a lot of time with Maw-Maw Fisher. She got to see the parts of me that Paw-Paw saw, and then she got to catch a glimpse of me slightly redeemed. I know she was proud. I know she was loved.

In early 2007, shortly after I shared a phone call with her to inform her of my new aspirations in life, Maw-Maw Fisher had a stroke that left her unable to speak. She was hospitalized for a long stretch of time and then moved across the road from the Pulaski hospital into the long-term rehab there. I visited almost every day. My error in failing to visit my Paw-Paw Largen was not going to occur again. Except for the DNA part of my being, I was a different person.

In September, on a Saturday morning, she passed away. I went to the hospital to see her vacant body lying there, with what is now the all too familiar look of the deceased, mouth agape, spirit gone.

One month before Maw-Maw Fisher died in 2007, I got another one of the types of phone calls that I got earlier in the year regarding Adam. This time it was my mom on the line telling me that Jason had died. Mom had served as a mother of sorts to Jason for a year or so in middle school when he practically lived with us in the basement apartment. Her heart was broken. "Overdose," she said. He and the girl he was hanging out with while his baby momma was serving a piece of jail time at the privatized palace, had gotten a room at one of the rundown motels in town. When they failed to check out, hotel staff found them both inside the room, deceased. Accidental overdose, times two.

It had not been long before that time that I saw Jason in the parking lot of Magic Mart (Appalachian type of Wal-Mart, which typically moved into smaller Wal-Mart buildings that closed when Supercenters were opened). My old friend was proudly holding his little girl outside of his aunt's car.

Maw-Maw Fisher and Others

Jason's daughter and Ella were similar in age. Upon hearing of his death my tears were for him, but more so for her. She would never really get to know her dad. He never knew his at all.

When the day of the funeral came, I put on the black pinstripe suit for the second time. At the church where the funeral was held, I encountered a lot of people from high school. Most of them could not believe I was there and healthy looking. I couldn't believe it either. In front of a large crowd in the large church off of Route 11, the preacher that day did a good job considering how tough of a situation this was. After the church service, we drove up to the Oakwood Cemetery to the far-right top of the hill that overlooks the giant and exquisite lot and home that I once dwelt, in a basement apartment. On that hill was the marker for his murdered brother Chris, and one for his mother Jennifer, and now one for Jason.

The next day I went to a church service in an old furniture store building with a guy I was sponsoring in N.A. He too was a close friend of Jason. I went to support him, and I had promised that one day I would check his church out. This was the day. I felt my blood boil as this preacher, who like me was in the church and at the graveside the day before, went on and on about Jason's death. At one point, he said, "And there stood his only living brother. The only one of those three children who remain. And I wanted to ask that young man, "Where do you want us to dig your hole?" Hearing such a thing coming out of the mouth of a pastor in such a moment was beyond frustrating to me. To be honest, I was furious. Not the place or the time to use the pulpit in such a way was my opinion. I wish I could say that he was wrong in his prophecy.

The youngest brother died in 2021. Aged thirty-three. He lived long past his brothers. I went by their home sometime after the youngest and last brother died. The remaining parts of the home that were not already ashes were covered in vines and other climbing weeds. You couldn't even see the porch on which we used to sit.

The next time one of those bad news types of phone calls came, Michael was on the other line. Keith was dead. He had been found in his room at his parent's home. An overdose caused by Methadone and benzos. It was early winter 2008. He was 26.

Keith had been doing well after getting out of jail the most recent time before his death. Then he found himself stricken with love for an attractive young woman who I had known to be someone who had also been a frequent customer at the Methadone clinic. One of the worst secrets of the recovery world is that addicts who are in recovery like to get romantically involved with other addicts in recovery. Seldom are the results of such getting together positive for either party. In this case, no matter how much "recovery" was going on, it certainly was not positive for Keith.

Once, Adam beat Keith up in the middle of Snider Ln. because he witnessed Keith hit his own mom in the eye. That was the first thing I thought of as I, outfitted in a brown suit, walked into the funeral home the night of his viewing and saw his grieving mother with tears rolling down her face. "He had a tough life," she said as I softly hugged her. I shook his dad's hand as he said, "I really thank you for coming, Jabe. Means a lot." I walked over and gazed down at my friend. There he was. Keefer we called him. He looked just fine. A troubled spirit who had struggled to find peace in life, had found it in death.

The next day, I donned my black pinstripe suit and went to the burial, where Keith was interned just a stone's throw from much of my family. The only living people in the cemetery I knew were his parents, aunt and uncle and cousins who I went to church with, and an older friend who used to live beside Keith and was like a big brother to him, Michael, and Adam. There weren't a lot of people there in general. There would have been more had they, too, not already found their way into the ground with a little help from pharmaceuticals.

27

Wall

AS IT TURNS OUT, and as I expected, my pastor who warned me about the difficulties of my journey to ordained leadership wasn't trying to be discouraging. He was being realistic. How I came into this realization is odd, however.

The person in charge of a geographical area within a conference of the United Methodist Church is known as a District Superintendent (DS). In some areas of the United Methodist Church, one of the first steps in becoming a pastor involves a conversation with the DS. After the conversation with my pastor, I set up my appointment with my DS at the time. We will call her Lois. Her voice reminded me of a Lois for some reason.

It was especially important given the circumstances surrounding my past that the conversation with Lois go well. I met her in her home one evening where I learned she was taking care of her granddaughter, ironically, I gathered, because the girl's parents were a lot like the previous version of me.

That night in Wytheville, VA, I laid out all my transgressions to Lois: addiction, arrests, driving violations, weekend incarcerations, on and on I went. One thing that I have identified as a character flaw, not always helpful in leadership, is that I can be prone to overshare (Which begs the question, "Why am I writing a memoir?").

That night with Lois, I felt it was imperative to live into my calling that I tell all, even if it was too much. Prior to leaving her parsonage that night, I was assured by Lois that all the stuff in my past could be overcome. She stated how grateful she was for my honesty. I was officially allowed to begin the process. The process involves a lot of hoops that require jumping.

Having her blessing to begin was a monumental first step for this kid from Pulaski.

A few weeks after our meeting, I received an email from Lois; my background check had come back. Apparently hearing about my past and reading about it caused two distinctly different reactions in the DS, Lois. At one point in the email (not phone call) she said, "I know God has the ability to change people's hearts, but in your case, I don't think it is possible." Not exactly a faithful or theological statement (trust me, I am no longer bitter). At another point she said, "I don't remember you telling me half of this." The truth was, I told her twice as much as what she read. The background check did a terrible job at capturing it all!

Because there is no singular decision maker in UMC polity at this point in the candidacy process, I was continuing on, yet now more discouraged than ever. Had it not been for a prayer once prayed in another discouraging moment I would have quit (and most likely turned Baptist). I was assigned a candidacy mentor, a United Methodist pastor of Jamaican descent. His name was Leroy, and he became my friend and ally. Leroy and I met each other on a regular basis in the fellowship hall of his church, which sat near to an all too familiar funeral home. There we would go through the mandated Candidacy Workbook, looking at my responses and discussing calling and ministry and a life of service in the name of both. At one point, early in our meetings, my Jamaican friend Leroy, rhythmically said, "Jabe, bruddah, they'r is not a doubt in myyy minda, You are called!"

On the day the District Committee on Ordained Ministry interviewed me and would vote on my certified candidacy, I sat in a room with several committee members for an hour of grilling, with Leroy constantly deflecting and redirecting questions in my favor. After the interview was complete, I was sent into the room next door to allow for the team to deliberate. The walls were paper thin. I listened to the discussion word for word. I could tell the consensus was that I was called into ministry. One voice rose, that of Lois, "Well, I guess if North Carolina wants him that bad, they can have him."

The question was called, "All in favor?" A room full of "Aye." I became a Certified Candidate for ministry in the United Methodist Church, allowing me to be eligible for a pastoral license and thus making myself available to pastor a church. When a wall appeared, God made an open window. All I had to do was be resilient enough to wait and crawl through. One crucial thing addictive addiction taught me by default was resiliency. One thing that I learned once I became clean is, if I do the right thing, even though "fairness" and "deserving" are not "things" from a perspective of grace, more times than not, good things happen.

28

Diapers

THE CERTIFICATION TO BE in ministry came in Spring 2011. Life had been changing rapidly and for the better. A couple of years after getting to Hickory Ave., with both Amber and I doing quite well, we realized we needed a bigger house, for two cats, and soon, a little baby boy, Isaiah (named for a scripture that mattered to his dad). In 2009, we found a house in Dublin (still Pulaski County) that was slightly bigger (about 1,000 sq. ft), and well accommodating for our soon to be family of four.

Isaiah William Derek came six weeks early, which required a stay at a NICU in Roanoke for a week. Seeing him for the first time as he was being rolled by in the incubator was an absolute overwhelming thrill. My heart flooded with emotion to see my first born (and only) son. My joy quickly turned to fear and confusion. I was not only afraid and confused but also heartbroken to hear that even though Isaiah was big and healthy, he had to stay in the NICU. To be honest, it took a few days to understand that it was for his own good. He had to have a little feeding tube in his nose for a few days, and then a few days after that he was homebound to Dublin.

By the time Isaiah was born, I was working for a company making railroad ties, as the 2008 housing market crash had swept away the job I loved making log home kits. Thankfully, the new company was much closer to Roanoke than Dublin, so I was able to see him every day, even when I had to work. It was a hard and stressful week on Amber and me, but soon we took our boy home. Our little family of four had blossomed.

Six months after Isaiah came home, we received quite surprising news when we were told that Amber was once again pregnant. This time, it would be another girl. We settled on the name Olivia for her. The middle names (all our children have two of those, thanks to their mom) had not yet been decided. One day while throwing a railroad switch to move rail cars at my job, I found one of those helium balloons that you really should not release up to the heavens to remember people or for any other purpose. This one had been released for the purposes of a Vacation Bible School experiment at a small-membership Baptist church in Kentucky. On the tag it said, "If found, contact Rebecca Cameron. . ." The same day we went to the now quite familiar high-risk neonatal office in Roanoke. As we got in the elevator, I looked at Amber and handed her the tag, "Olivia Rebecca Cameron," I said. It stuck. The name, not the elevator.

Olivia came in November 2022. Unlike Isaiah's birth that I could not attend due to Amber having to be put under, and unlike Ella's where the same concept applied but I could have seen through glass had I not been distracted, I was able to be in the OR for Olivia's birth and to cut the umbilical cord. The child came out screaming and red. She did not stop screaming for days. Amber and I, at least once a day for the few days we were there, would beg the nurses to take her to the nursery so we could get some rest, her in the hospital bed, I on the fold-out hospital couch.

I do not cherish sentimental things. I do cherish some photos. The photo of all 3 of our children sitting together on a Radford hospital couch, down the hall from the mental portion of the hospital that saved my life, is a photo that is deeply meaningful for me. All I have to do is close my eyes to see it.

During this hospitalization, as we and the hospital staff were preparing for the birth of Olivia, I made a tremendous mistake. I talked Amber into having her tubes tied. We knew we did not want to have other children, but she was not exactly excited with the idea in that moment; yet finally we agreed to have the doctor perform the operation following Olivia's delivery.

It should have been me. I should have done what needed to be done to prevent adding a fourth to our crew. I believe it was a sadness with the tube decision combined with some postpartum problems that led Amber to have another psychosis just a month after Olivia was born. Thankfully, this time she was able to go to the Radford Hospital's St. Alban's wing, and not back to Salem. I was taking night classes for my undergrad degree in the basement below where she stayed. I visited almost every day that I could, while also working, commuting, and taking care of the three kids, obviously with a lot of good family help.

Just before this episode, Amber and I had visited Duke University's Divinity School in September and agreed there was probably no chance in Hades I would ever get accepted into their Master of Divinity program. For starters, I had no prior theological training. I was a hillbilly man, not far removed from being an overgrown boy, who was finishing undergrad in a makeshift classroom in the basement of a hospital. Oh, and I had been arrested and used to shoot up dope.

On our visit to the Duke campus, I walked into the school and asked an unassuming, kind-ish looking man if he knew where we might find the Divinity School. He looked at me from head to toe, seemingly shocked that I did not know who he was, and said, "You're in it, buddy." I would later learn that man was the school's most well-known theologian, Stanley Hauerwas.

Soon after the visit, once again, God made a way. I was accepted to Duke Divinity School. When the call came in, life was so painful and chaotic, we were not able to celebrate. Once Amber got better, we tried to make up for the lack of celebration while at the same time coming to the realization that if we were going to do this, some hard things were about to happen. Namely, leaving our families, and being the first in either family to do such. No one in my family had completed college, much less moved away.

It was a big ask on my part. After all, I was the only one who had a prayer in a pickup promising God I would take the next step and the next and the next until there was no longer a way. Amber, nor any of the kids had asked for such a drastic move and life change. Nor, as I said, did we expect it would ever happen. I mean, I wrote my essay on what theologian had formed me most on Max freaking Lucado. No offense Max, it's just others at that school write about Barth, Bonhoeffer, Julian of Norwich, Augustine, Ellen Davis, Richard Hayes, Thomas Aquinas, and folks like that, not on (very helpful) coffee table theology. I wrote just well enough and presented well enough on my visit that I got in somehow. Now with the opportunity there, we had to decide, do we move?

After looking at our options around Durham and seeing the impossibilities of my being a full-time student only, Amber and I decided that should I receive a Student Pastor appointment which would provide us with income and housing, we would have our confirmation that moving was right. In the Spring of 2011, Amber and I made the trek to Duke so I could interview for a student pastorate. Back in those days, there were a lot of Student Pastor appointments in the area around Duke. These appointments were mostly in rural churches, and all of them being United Methodist churches.

It is important to note that only the Methodist tradition uses the word "appointment" to name the assignment of a pastor to a parish. This came about in the 18th century in America when pastors rode on horses around on "circuits" from church to church. Each circuit had 2 pastors, and each church within that circuit had an "assigned time" that the pastor would roll through (or gallop in) on their given day, hence "appointments." I was not willing to ride a horse, but I was willing to take on as many churches as needed to be able to go to seminary and feed my family/buy diapers simultaneously.

The competition was obviously fierce, and there were only so many appointments, and more desiring an appointment than there were places to put them. As mentioned prior, in the United Methodist way of organization, a District Superintendent (DS) serves as the leader of geographical regions that contain a great number of churches. One of the responsibilities of the DS is to aid in the appointment of pastors in the churches in their area. When there are churches that have historically welcomed student pastors for their four years of study, it is the DS's job to work with Duke to interview those who are willing to serve while in school and to try and find the right matches. On the day of the interviews, I was selected to interview with four DS's. Two were from North Carolina and two were from across the state line, north of Durham in Virginia.

The first interview was with one of the North Carolina folks and it went well, I could tell he liked me. So much so that at the end of the interview he said, "The church I am here looking for today is in Unnamed County. But if you have kids, you don't want them to go to school in Unnamed County. I cannot in good conscience put you in Unnamed County although I think you are a great fit for this church."

The next two DS's were from the Virginia Conference. Each had one church in mind just off Interstate 85. Both DS's were kind, and both said something to the effect of, "You probably don't want to make that long of a drive. But if you don't find anywhere else by the end of April, give me a call."

The final interview was with a DS named Chuck Cook. I walked into this very old room in the Gray building at Duke Divinity (named for a person, but the place exudes grayness naturally) to find Chuck playing away masterfully on a grand piano. I have yet to go to an opera, but I imagine at the one with the phantom fellow, the music sounds much akin to the beautiful noise Chuck was making that afternoon. I stood to the side of Chuck, his flat-top haircut, and the piano; a good distance away, but close enough to be seen. To this day I don't know if he kept playing for another two minutes because he didn't see me, or because he did see me.

Once the music stopped, the questioning began. None of the other interviewers asked such hard Methodism-based doctrinal questions. It would be years before I could answer the types of questions he was asking. After all, that is why I was going to Duke in the first place, to learn. Throughout the thing, Chuck seldom smiled, and he seemed genuinely unimpressed by the hillbilly who sat before him.

At the conclusion of the interview, I lumbered around the Gray building, getting lost in one maze after another, until finally finding the familiar spot outside where Amber waited. "How'd it go?" she asked. To which I replied, "There is one person in life I will never have call me for anything, especially an appointment: Chuck Cook."

I had managed to live through all I had lived through. Had beaten all sorts of odds, the law, the needle, all the while cheating death, yet on a Spring day in Durham, NC, I ran into something I could not overcome, a military man turned United Methodist preacher, turned DS.

A couple weeks later, the phone rang, "Hello, Jabe. Chuck Cook here."

29

Where? What?

When Chuck called, I was not only shocked, but I was also elated. This was it. This was God opening a vitally important door/window or whatever it is God opens to allow possibilities to become realities. Chuck said he had a two-point charge (two smaller membership churches that share a pastor and the responsibility of paying their salary and providing housing) that was in Such and Such County. I didn't care if they were on the moon, I would commute however far I had to commute, and in the case of these two charges it would be an hour one way. I thanked my former phantom foe repeatedly until finally he bid me adieu with an assurance that I would be hearing from him real soon.

Weeks went by. The time to call the Virginia folks back came and went. One day the phone rang. "Hi Jabe, my name is Doug, and my church in Durham is looking for a youth pastor. I got your name from a list of people who came to student pastor day who still do not have an appointment." "Whoa, whoa, whoa," I said. "Chuck Cook said that I not only have one church, but I have two. I don't understand why my name is on your list."

"Oh," he said. "I'm just letting you know you are on there. So, I take it you don't wish to interview."

"No."

I called Chuck Cook as fast as the Roadrunner says, "*meep, meep*." Brother Cook advised me that everything was alright and to calm down and to trust God. Calm down! This was no matter to play around with. Dag-nab-it, God opened the window, who gave Chuck Cook the right to close it? "Trust God" he said. I thought, I trust God aplenty, but its Chuck Cook that I am not so sure about.

A week later, while in a large lift truck moving crossties around the railyard at work, my phone rang, and it was Chuck. "Jabe, I am calling to let you know that you are being appointed to Faison United Methodist Church. They have a parsonage, and you can move in on June 28. Alright. See you soon, we will go to visit. Bring the family. We will eat pizza before we go."

Faison was not in Such and Such County, and it was only one church. But like I said, the moon would have been ok too. I hopped out the lift truck and screamed with all my might with so much satisfaction and relief. I even danced a little, while fist pumping the air. All those years of sorrow and struggle. All those years of grief and pain. All those years of destruction and destitution. Near homelessness, no electricity, no food, fourteen jobs at that point, funerals, oh so many funerals (still to this day no Pulaski friend's weddings), the weekend nights on a cold concrete floor, all the madness and mayhem, the car wrecks, and the needle, and the psychoses, Miriam, Paw-Paw, Maw-Maw, all of that and so much more. All the grace. Grace on top of grace. Finally, something my parents and remaining grandparents could be proud of. Finally, potential, recognized and realized.

All that needed to be done after talking to Chuck was to eat the pizza with him, meet my church, load a truck, and learn how to be a pastor and a Duke student for the next four years. The night after the pizza, and for many years later, the church showed us nothing but love.

The toughest part of seminary was not the 89.6-mile one way drive each day (I quickly made a new best friend named Kyle who I carpooled with who made that drive/ride bearable). The toughest part was, there was no one there like me. I mean, there were other people there who had lived through hardships. I'm not pretentious enough to find myself unique. Geographically speaking, there were not hillbillies there like me who had also been through some stuff like I had. Also, I had not been in a traditional learning environment since the first semester of 11th grade, and to be honest, because of my levels of intoxication in high school, the argument could be made that the last time I had truly been "present" in a traditional learning environment was in middle school.

The people I was meeting were different. They had been doing this school thing for a long time and they, unlike me, had been doing it at a very high level. Their language was different. They knew a lot of words. They used a lot of words I did not even know how to spell. They talked about scholars I had never heard of. To be honest, I didn't know what a scholar was at first. During my first week, my friends from back home would have kicked the crap out of this one kid for correcting me as he did, when I said Karl Barth with the "th" as opposed to the proper saying of "Bart." Why the hell is the "h" there then Brandon?

I had written enough in obtaining my first two degrees to know that I was a decent enough writer. I had also worked for a season at the local newspaper while I was still using. I started covering sports, then news, and then they let me write commentaries (all of this while fighting the nods dosed up on Methadone, with a newspaper in the history room located near my desk that named me as a fugitive of justice). This seminary writing was different though. I would write papers I felt were solid only to get them back with numbers like "70" written on them as they were covered in red ink. Maybe I had bitten off more than I could chew. Maybe God forgot to close the window.

One of the worst parts of my life story is that I shot dope and did all manners of narcotics. One of the most useful parts of my life story that helped me to make it through one of the world's most prestigious seminaries is that I shot dope and did all manners of narcotics. To be an addict, you must survive in all sorts of ways. Sometimes through your own devices, and sometimes with the help of others. Always with a good measure of Divine grace. Unmerited of course, as all grace is.

Being a "good" addict also requires the ability to adapt. The ability to pursue something relentlessly. The ability to utilize shenanigans as needed to obtain what it is that you are out to obtain. The ability to do whatever it takes.

It took four grinding years of adapting and pursuing, and a lot of support from Amber. For example, during the first year, a typical week would look like this for us: Each morning, Monday through Thursday, I would wake up and leave for Durham before the sun rose. Amber would get up, get Ella (7), Isaiah (not quite 2) and Olivia (not even 1) up and ready. The two smallest ones would go to the daycare, Ella would be dropped off too, so that she could get a ride to school when the school opened for students to enter. Amber would drive to the next county over where she taught middle school science.

After the school day ended, she would pick the three back up at the daycare, run the errands that needed running, return home and cook and change diapers and do all other manners of housekeeping. I would return, hopefully before dark depending on the time of year. I would eat, hold my children, and pray that no pastoral emergencies arose. The rhythm became easier as the years went on. I cook 95% of the meals at home these days. This is partly out of the joy of the task, and then in another part as a means of gratitude for some tough years that did not have to be as tough had I not answered the call.

Getting me to the end of the Duke journey with a successful completion also took a lot of good teachers, a lot of support from the Faison church and community, the brotherhood with Kyle and our other student pastor friends, a lot of student loans, and a scholarship earned after year one. Because of all that support, and a great measure of grace, the hillbilly they call Jabe, with the scar tissue on his arm, walked across the chancel area of big and beautiful, stone-structured Duke Chapel to receive a degree and a Masters hood. You better believe I had a lot of folks walking with me who had never even heard of Duke Chapel. Mom and dad and Amber were able to be there to witness it. It was just as much their doing as it was mine. They were all three over the moon proud for not only what I had achieved, but for what we had achieved together.

Six years later that same hillbilly would earn the right to be called Doctor. I didn't walk across a stage that time. A global pandemic happened.

30

Faison

FAISON IS A TOWN in rural Eastern North Carolina that was founded the same year the United States declared its independence. Faison is a community that has for years served as an agricultural stalwart in the state of North Carolina and beyond. For much of the 20th century, Faison was well known for its produce market. Wholesalers would line up and down the road by the produce market to pick up product being sold within the market's area. As the economy in the United States began to change from a regional to a more national and then global one, the produce market closed and made way for large produce distribution companies in and around the town.

In addition to the produce growers and distributors, there are also those who maintain family run farms, that have tended the land in Faison for generations. These folks, many my friends, grow row crops such as soybeans, corn, cotton, and peanuts. These products are sold to conglomerate corporations who now completely control not only the price, but most other aspects that go into the grower's operation.

This is especially the case for those who have contracts for the use of their chicken, turkey, or hog houses, in which the farmer is responsible for the upkeep of the house for the corporations' products (the animals). The corporate folks hire managers who travel from house to house checking on things and providing guidance as to how much feed is to be given, and when other manners of treatment to promote the growth of the animal are needed. Many around Faison find their being in roles such as the manager role, or in some other form of service and support for the agricultural work.

March to November, a large number of migrant workers return to the Faison area as they are integral to the produce portion of the agricultural economy. These workers can be found on any given day, depending on the season, picking strawberries, blueberries, eggplants, varieties of squash, or digging up sweet potatoes. For many years it was the case, that if you had yams on Thanksgiving, chances are Faison soil was to thank.

On our moment of arrival in Faison, we were welcomed by a whole cast of folks from the church. They greeted us with open arms and treated us with lots of food. Not just food, good food. Locally grown food as well. A few guys who were migrant workers working with one of the distribution companies came to help unload the moving truck that I had almost single-handedly loaded myself, on up until 4:00 the morning of our trek to Duplin County. Once the truck was unloaded with their help and some of the help of people like Brad and Rusty who would become some of my very best friends in life, the Largen five settled in and made Faison home, with our two cats, and now, since it was allowed, two dogs.

As tough as it was on me, I love Pulaski dearly. It is home. Faison quickly became home as well. I still consider it such although I no longer reside there. The bonds of friendship and love there are deep. Are there some there who are glad that I am gone? Absolutely! Are there some folks I am glad I do not have to see or deal with anymore? Absolutely! It is hard to make a place home for ten years and not endure some relational hardships, or hardships in general; twenty years of life in Pulaski County had already taught me that. In my experience, it is the avoidance of conflict that causes many in pastoral ministry to flounder.

In terms of our ministry in Faison, there was little floundering. I believe my internal desire to excel in ministry was born out of my wanting to "balance" the ledger of my life that had been in the negative column for far too long.

In the early years after arrival, worship attendance grew greatly. We became stable enough financially that by the time I graduated Duke we were able to move from a student pastor appointment to a full-time appointment. Our reach in the community was far. At one point, we won a denominational award for our level of, and success with, community engagement.

We began a summer food program that later added pandemic food program to its purview. We opened a thrift shop that sought to operate more like a "sharing shop" as opposed to a place of business. It was located right on the corner of town near the red light. Our name and logo for all passing through to see.

When options for a quality pre-K program outside of the competitive school system program were seemingly none, we began the Mustard Seed Christian Academy Preschool. Later, I would take the initiative to lead the building of a soccer field, with a tremendous amount of help from the community, and on one of the community's most sacred pieces of land, the former produce market. Thankfully, due to the commitment of the laity and the town leadership, except for the thrift shop, all these community minded ministries remain intact at the time of this writing.

Faison was the perfect home for our family for a decade. We loved all the perks of Duplin County life. The park and ball field and gym at the center of the community. The sharing of good food from gardens and larger fields. The tasty goodness made by Ms. Nhut, a Vietnamese woman beloved by all who know her, who makes some of the world's best soul food at her café. The kindness of the people. The way that our family became a part of so many other families in just a short amount of time. The sunsets.

Faison was the perfect place for me to learn how to be a pastor as well. It is there that I learned how to lead. It is there that I learned how to preach. It is there I learned how to teach. It is there that I learned how to navigate conflict. It is there that I learned to take things that I had learned in my education and utilize them in faithful and fruitful ways with good folks alongside. It is there that I graduated seminary and received a doctoral degree. It is there that I was ordained.

It was there that I constantly had to deal, in a new capacity, with an old foe named Death.

31

She

IN MY FOUR YEARS of student pastoring, and then in the six years of full-time pastoring that followed, I made a lot of friends in Faison. If I were to list all those who I hold dear to this day, the list would require its own chapter. One friendship looms large in my consciousness, due in large part because of her death, and the toll it took on my spirit, mind, and ultimately, my body. Our friendship was an unlikely thing to say the least. She was in her mid-sixties when the friendship started. I was barely thirty.

She was the one, when we first moved into the parsonage in 2011, who would drive by slowly, head cocked, making observations, every day for the first week or two that we were there. By the way, she nor anyone she needed to visit lived on that street. Later, it would be her mother's landscaper who would scout while on the golf cart and then report back to her.

She was also the one I overheard complaining about me allowing popcorn in the sanctuary for a movie night during my first year of ministry. When I stepped into the church kitchen and confronted her about what I heard her saying, she barked back and stood her ground. She then called me that night to apologize, telling me how much she loved me and my family. I apologized as well, and said, "I love you too."

On the night in which we had a contemporary Christian band concert, and I shared my testimony for the first time, it was she who first met me at the bottom of the large flatbed trailer's steps to hug me and tell me I was loved. Over the period of six years, she became one of the greatest friends of my entire life.

I received a call from her one Friday while leaving the golf course (golf is a game I, sometimes regrettably, got seriously involved with upon moving to Faison). She said, "Now, Jabe, don't get upset. . .". Strangely, but truly, my first thought was about popcorn. The next word that I heard and understood snapped me out of that, I heard her say "cancer."

The entire tone of my voice changed as I began to question what she had just said. She said it was going to be alright, she was leaving her regular doctor and making her way to the oncologist to set up her appointments there. It was small-cell lung cancer, the same kind that had killed Paw-Paw. I met her at the oncologist in about fifteen minutes time. I, among others, held her hand in the waiting room and hugged her in the parking lot.

Months went by and she seemed to be doing ok, all things considered. Other people loved her too. The community of Faison, as it always does, surrounded her and her elderly mother with love. She lost her hair and had a couple of scary fainting episodes. One occurred while standing beside me in the sanctuary. The other happened at her mother's home, I with some other friends, answered the call to help get her up and to convince her to take a ride in the rescue squad truck.

One day she asked me to come and visit, and I did so at her mom's where she had moved in so that they could care for one another. Her mother stayed in the room next door, as my friend cried and lamented. "Why? Who is going to take care of mom? Why would God allow this to happen now? Why can't I stay well long enough to care for my mother? She shouldn't have to care for me. I feel as if God has abandoned me." She knew the cigarettes were the reason why, but her lack of feeling that God was doing anything about this was a valid questioning given her current situation.

Lament. The verbalizing of one's disdain for the way things are and God's role or lack thereof in the way things are. That's what Jesus was doing from the cross as he quoted the opening lines from a Psalm of Lament, Psalm 22. It was what my friend was doing in that living room in Faison, NC. It's ok to do. Sometimes, it is necessary. Four years at Duke taught me that when we join the cries of "My God, my God," at least we are acknowledging "my God."

It was only a couple of weeks later when my friend called me back over. She said, "I had a dream, and I want to tell you about it." She and I both sat in the same spots that we had been in for the previous conversation. She said that in this dream, she had a vision of Christ. Christ was standing outside of a tomb, and his arms were stretched out wide (what was left of her body mimicked what Christ was doing in the vision). She then said, "That told me everything was going to be alright. Jesus showed me everything is going to be alright." For her, in that moment, it was a vision of healing and restoration in the now of that moment. Not some far-off, future salvation. A salvation of the now. I would agree, but I would also add it is now, *and* it is later.

That sit down was in mid-summer. Right before autumn began, I was called to a local hospital where she was in excruciating pain. I stayed until they transferred her to the other hospital, where she could receive better care. I hugged her and reminded her that everything was going to be alright just as Christ had showed her.

The next morning, I woke up and went to her bedside in a fourth-floor room overlooking the front parking lot of the hospital. I stayed there talking to her, now with her unable to reply. There were a couple others in the room with us that day, loving and caring, but unique characters too. At one point when the room emptied, I stood at the foot of her bed and said, "You know how much I love you. It is obvious how much I love you if I am willing to stay here with those two." She would have laughed if she could.

A little while later, while one of the others went to get her mom and bring her up, the nurse rolled my friend's body over from her left side to her right. Shortly after that turning, she breathed her last. Her eyes open, fixed on me.

During our conversation about her dream, we also talked about what was to happen when her breath gave out. She was adamant, saying repeatedly, "No church funeral. Graveside only. Just tell them about Jesus at the graveside and make sure that is it. I mean it, Jabe. Graveside only. Just talk about Jesus."

At the graveside, I did just that. I talked about Jesus. Life, death, resurrection. Just as promised. But I also told the crowd gathered among the weathered tombstones of the Faison Cemetery about a dream that a good friend of mine had. Where in telling me about it, all eight-five pounds of her demonstrated what the Christ by the grave had revealed to her through holding his arms up and out wide. And I held mine up, just as all eighty-five pounds of her had done weeks before. Everything was going to be alright.

Her death had been the second one in the church that week. The other was a man who was very special and beloved as well. His death would have been enough to bear on its own for the week. After having one of my best friends die staring at me, I had enough. "I'm too emotional of person, who gets attached to these people too easily," was what I had started telling myself.

At one point the day that my beloved friend died, I stepped out of her room and into the hallway. From there, I called my mom through rivers of tears. I told her how I felt I did not have it in me to do things such as this. "I don't think I can do this. I don't think I can watch her die." To which my mom replied, "You are supposed to be there." I had heard that before in a sad situation surrounded by a cloud of death. This time, it was the voice of my mother with the assurance. The assurance did not make anything easier, but it reminded me of my calling. A calling that often requires a stare down with death.

About two years prior to her death, I had started drinking alcohol casually and socially after nearly ten years of no drugs or alcohol whatsoever. I figured I was a new creation and given my many successes in ministry and knowing many others in ministry who partook, I figured I could handle it. Our church was growing, I had become not only a church leader but also a community leader. In ways measurable and immeasurable, the Faison church, and the community activities I was a part of were thriving. Why couldn't I handle a little alcohol from time to time? It seemed like everyone else I knew (for the most part) could.

The days and weeks after my beloved friend's death was the first major clue that I could not handle drinking successfully. It would take several years to admit it.

The Friday after she died, I gathered with a group of friends. That night I drank an entire fifth of whiskey by myself. Late in the night, when nobody was looking, I wept. My months of "casual" and "social" drinking had conditioned me to the point of reaching the next level, a level I knew all too well. That night and in the days to follow, I reached it. This cycle of turning to the drink in a heavy fashion amid death became a habit, and an unhealthy one at that. I wish I could say that the grip of the drink in hard times came upon me like a thief in the night. It didn't. I should not have been surprised, in fact, I wasn't. Ashamed, but not surprised.

32

Ashes

MANY HARD TO DEAL with deaths happened in the Faison years. Not all of them happened in Faison, however. Some were back in the hills.

The bond between my dad and Maw-Maw Largen was a strong one. It was no secret that Maw-Maw and dad were close, and conversely Paw-Paw and J.W. were close. Maw-Maw was a byproduct of the beautiful rolling hills and mountain vistas of Floyd County, VA. Floyd is now well known for its annual gathering of hippies and such at an event in a field dubbed Floyd Fest. When Maw-Maw was born, hippie was not in the vernacular and Floyd County was predominantly an agricultural community where neighbors depended upon neighbors, and families worked hard to provide as much of their own provision as possible.

She was born Melva Lucille Keith, daughter of Jabe and Hattie Keith. My namesake died not long after my birth. Granny Hattie was around for several years of my life. She would send me $1 each year on my birthday. She was an exceptionally kind woman who lived during the end of the 19th century, and through most of the 20th. Granny Hattie was at one time a schoolteacher in one of the schools created through the leadership of the charismatic Rev. Bob Childress on the Buffalo Mountain.

Melva met James Largen and they wed. First came J.W. and then her beloved Sammy. In the late 70's and early 80's, Sammy meets Sherry, they are wed, and a boy is born in a little hospital in Radford. One of the wishes of Jabe Keith was that one of his descendants carry forth his name. I was the last chance while he was living.

Not long after our exodus from Pulaski, Maw-Maw Largen found out she had bone cancer. She tried chemo once and became so ill, she decided that was not what she wanted for the rest of her life. With no one remaining who could help care for her in the home, the decision was made for her to enter a nursing facility. Dad and J.W. kept watch with her every day. She was there far longer than anyone expected. The time drug on slowly.

We would visit and take her great-grandchildren to visit as often as we could. This was one of the things we knew we would have to deal with when windows kept opening and we had to move. Knowing a thing is a thing does not diminish the reality of having to deal with the thing when you encounter the thing. Finally, death came calling with peace in one hand and compassion in the other. All the weeping I did in the parking lot outside of the nursing home following visits had taken care of my grief. When the time came, I was relieved.

Paw-Paw Fisher was born around the same time as Maw-Maw Largen. His family endured the Great Depression as good as a family in Pulaski could. He was born with a defect that caused one side of his body to be smaller than the other. That did not stop him from being a hard worker. He worked at Coleman's Furniture and then Pulaski Furniture and then Ethan Allen, for a total of approximately fifty years. In my view, he was the epitome of a good man. Kind, smart, sweet, funny, caring.

Once, as a little boy, Paw-Paw Fisher, then only known as Johnny, was summoned to the family outhouse by his older brothers. There, at the bottom of the outhouse hole was a rat. The brothers advised little Johnny to run into the house, grab the family shotgun and then come back to exterminate the rodent. Johnny did just as they said. He stuck the barrel of the shotgun down the hole, hovered the gun's open end above where the rat remained, pulled the trigger and *KABOOM, SPLUSH, SPLATTER*. There stood little Johnny covered in the family business. He was a great storyteller. And obviously, way too good of a listener.

The day my mom found out she was pregnant with me is the same day that Paw-Paw had a massive heart attack and died. Thanks to good physicians and a major heart procedure at a hospital far, far away he was brought back to life, more than once, and then given the right number of by-passes to keep him going. It was also on this same day, that Maw-Maw Fisher's mother passed away. Needless to say, the day my birth was announced was quite a memorable day for the Fisher side of the family. In the literary world, some may say that day was "foreshadowing."

Giving up cigarettes, making some dietary changes, and continuing to work kept Paw-Paw alive for a great number of years. He and my mom were what we call a bonded pair. After Maw-Maw was gone, and mom no longer with Randy, she moved back into her childhood home that was also his childhood home. The two of them became like peas and carrots. It was a beautiful relationship to behold. Eventually his heart gave out. Unfortunately for my grief, I had not cried for him already. When we drove from Faison and Olivia and I entered his home, the pain of his loss buckled me.

My Uncle J.W. was master of shenanigans long before his nephew came along. He had a taste for all the things that intoxicate: a taste that never quenched for any significant amount of time. His marriage did not work out, leaving him to live in his childhood home for many years with Maw-Maw and Paw-Paw, and then in his final years on his own.

He was a master fisherman, and hunter (not just dope, actual animals). He kept company with a woman from Roanoke who I considered to be an Aunt. I envied his freedom and lack of responsibilities. Another hero, no doubt.

J.W. worked the second shift at a sock factory for several years, until it moved out of town and into another country. He liked the second shift because he could get off, party and/or fish all night long, and then sleep it off come morning, just in time to make his next shift. When many of my friends, including Adam, Michael and Winky began working at the sock factory on nights after school, I quickly learned of my Uncle's tendency to be just like me. Or was it vice versa? Or does it matter, genetically speaking?

His struggles became even more apparent when Amber, Ella and I were living in the Hickory Ave. house. Walleye (J.W.'s nickname), showed up with a very rare, expensive, German made .22 rifle. He gave me a big speech about how he wanted me to have it, prior to handing it over and stumbling back to his truck. The next day, my dad called and told me about how J.W. had been in a tizzy. He woke up, went out to his truck, noticed his gun missing, ran inside and began to yell, "Somebody stole my damn gun!" I laughed as dad told me about the happenings and then informed him, I had the gun, as it was gifted to me last night. I took the gun back up on the hill. The four of us remaining Largen's had a talk. I was grateful this time I was not the one in the chair of shame. Around this same time frame, someone broke into my truck parked outside of the house on Hickory and stole a rare German knife Walleye had given me.

Another incident occurred about a year after the gun incident. J.W. had purchased an older model Jaguar car from someone local. It was a beautiful burgundy color with lots of shiny chrome. It purred like a kitten.

The leather on the inside was a rich, deep tan. He let Amber and I take it on a date to the Red Lobster in Christiansburg one night. We rolled around in that thing like we were somebody. Not long after date night, J.W. lost the car in a game of poker. Much like what happened with the .22, he didn't remember that important detail from the night before. A few days later, much to the surprise of Maw-Maw and my dad (and maybe J.W. too) a very angry man we did not know showed up and took the car, after a bit of confrontation.

Before the COVID 19 pandemic happened, J.W. learned that he had some internal, physical issues that were not going to get better. It was not long before he required the same type of full-time residential care that Maw-Maw had once required. The closest nursing facility with an open bed was over an hour away. No one could visit due to the facilities rules in response to the pandemic. He died alone. No one could keep watch with him. Dad wanted to. As, did I.

His body was cremated. We placed his ashes at his daddy's feet.

As was my custom in those days, I tried to fill my hidden wounds with a liquid substance that has no capacity to heal or fill any sort of woundedness. With each sip, wounds only widen. Needless to say, my beloved uncle and I were cut from the same cloth in more ways than one.

33

Darkness

For most of my adult life, depression had been just a word. Like other words, I knew it's meaning. As I matured and became active in ministry, I learned that depression was something that all sorts of people dealt with. I had known friends, like Rocky, and family members, like my cousin Wally, who had taken their own lives. I came to understand that depression was a serious thing, but it wasn't until depression came for me that I began to fathom the darkness and pain it entails.

My first real bout of depression came shortly after my beloved Faison friend died. Unlike the predictability of my dive into drinking amidst death once I started, depression came upon me like a thief in the night. I did not know what to call what I was experiencing. I just knew it was causing me to not be myself. Over the years of coming through United Methodist pastoral ministry, you must take a lot of assessments pertaining to your personality type. One is the Enneagram assessment. I am primarily an Enneagram "3". One trait of a "3" is you like to get things done. Beginning in 2017, and on and off until 2020, I found myself not caring to get things done. I found myself wanting to stay in bed for extended periods of time. I found myself feeling as if life was not worth the living. I pondered the thought of joining so many others I had known in whatever happens next when the breath stops.

In early 2020, right before the COVID-19 was declared an emergency, I finally went to see the doctor who seemed to not admire the three years of what I thought were heroic battles through depression and the need for achievement fueled bounce backs. During that stretch of time, I had enrolled in a Doctor of Ministry program through the Candler School of

Theology at Emory University. I was bored with ministry and needed to achieve something. I needed a renewed sense of purpose; something to fill a void. In those early months of 2020, not even the doctoral program was enough to keep me out of the depths of my depression. I couldn't fully get out of it during this season. On my best days, I was still wading in it. After a return trip from Atlanta, the medical doctor said I needed medicine. He was right. I sought out and saw a therapist too.

I began to feel much better and made it from early 2020 to early 2021 without any major depressive episode. I no longer pondered death, and I felt as if I was becoming a more productive person again.

Amber had gone through a lot during the stretch of 2020 – 2021. A month-long stint in rehab gave her a fresh start in life without alcohol, which was desperately needed. Shortly after that, since her psychiatric doctor had taken her off her medication due to the drinking, she required another hospital stay. The TDO equivalent in the state of North Carolina is an Involuntary Commitment (IVC). It would take one of those for her to get the needed help.

She bounced back quick, and things seemed to settle for us both. Oddly, perhaps, I found myself less dependent on a strong drink during heartbreaking, death involved days when Amber was sober and well. This renewed household health seemed to help my mental well-being. Turns out, pouring a depressant into your body in the name of numbness and feeling well, does not help depression.

Thinking I was now in the clear, and perhaps immune to another period of depression since I had the medicine's help, a healthier home, and a rejuvenated approach to life, I was shocked when slowly I crept back, even further, into darkness. In the Hebrew tradition, there is a place of despair in the depths called *Sheol*. In my depression, I felt like I was there, with no feasible way out that I could see.

One thing that I have come to discover about my depression, be I drinking or not, is that I can predict when I am about to enter fully into it. The indicator is a dissatisfaction with where I am. When I begin to get on job search websites, or start searching up other places to live, I am depressed or will soon be. The irony is that my doctoral project centered around clergy having appreciation for their place and love for their place and not wanting to be in any other place, so that they can be fully present and lead well in their context. As I was nearing the completion of that work, I found myself questioning my place and my vocation. Good people like my advisor Dr. Alison Collis Greene were vital during this time of wrestling, struggle, and discernment. I was just connected enough, to conversation partners, like Alison and my friend Kyle, to keep from going completely under. Like that day in Claytor Lake twenty-five years prior, I could still feel my head going down deeper and back up lower with each trip downward.

At the time this newest darkness was approaching and beginning to settle, I was also blessed to be under the tutelage of Dr. Greg Ellison (he would call it something more like a partnership in learning). Dr. Ellison had a way of making me contemplate many things that needed contemplating, which typically is good for me. When struggling with depression and trying to determine whether my life had meaning, is not, in my experience, the greatest time to do a Howard Thurman-esq meditation of the heart or deep dive of the soul. It never felt good anyway. It may have been good. Feelings are not always facts.

On a Tuesday in early 2021, I made a solo trip to a pizza place one town over. Throughout the ten years we lived in Faison, I had been to this pizza place many times. My presence there was especially frequent during COVID, as the owner agreed to be one of the local businesses that would partner with us to feed the children in our portion of the county who were no longer getting lunch meals. The concept was simple, we (the church) would help the small business eateries in our area with business in a time in which they were not getting much, and all they had to do is to stay open, pay their employees, and make the food the children needed.

On the Tuesday I took the trip to the pizza place for personal business, I had really been struggling mentally. My outlook was grim. Intrusive thoughts continued to enter my mind. One such thought that I was familiar with was veering over in the next lane and allowing a feed truck or some other large vehicle to do for me what I wished to be done. My conscience always rebelled against that thought. I would not want to have someone live the rest of their life, knowing they were behind the wheel on the other side. One thing about intrusive thoughts, they intrude. Intruders, by definition, come when they are not invited or wanted. Thank God for a conscience that operated like a guard dog, keeping the intruder at bay.

I pulled into the drive-thru at the pizza place. The wait was long. When I finally reached the window, I was greeted by an employee I had never seen before. This was odd given the number of times I had been there during our COVID response. His face was full of piercings. His hair was unkempt and coming out of lots of places and going lots of ways out from under a ragged hat, covered in flour dust. His eyes had the look of a maniac, his voice was equally maniacal. In an instant, he became for me one of those characters that I had read about in Flannery O'Connor stories. He was a maniac who would lead me to an epiphany. It was getting ready to be a strange encounter with grace.

As he handed me our pizzas, his wild eyes met mine as he awkwardly and loudly proclaimed, "Paid for. Already paid for." I inquired as to whether the owner had arranged this (he had before). "Nope. That's not what it is. Paid for." He laughed. I pulled away and wept the rest of the way home.

Were I not in ministry, I would not be able to do the things that I do like feed hungry children. Were I not alive, I would not be able to be recipient of gifts, nor the giver of them. Were I not alive, I would not have the opportunity to experience moments such as the one I had just experienced, where a wild-eyed, unkempt maniac kept me in ministry and potentially saved a life; mine. It was time to go see my doctor again. My dose needed a boost. I was no longer ashamed to admit it. In a strange ironic turn, pills once took my life, almost completely. Many years later, pills save my life. The key is: "Use as directed."

The day after the pizza drive thru, I stayed online after class to tell Dr. Ellison and his assistant what had happened. He knew I had been struggling. Following a conversation about my encounter, vocation, depression, and life, in his wisdom, Dr. Ellison concluded our time by remarking, "How strange grace can be when it comes to you in the form of a madman and free pizza." We three laughed like crazy.

Life. Paid for. Already paid for.

34

Bethany Revisited

Leaving Faison after ten years of homemaking was a heartbreaking thing to do. Ten years of ministry and sharing life is a significant amount of time, especially for a United Methodist pastor. At the time we left, Amber and I had spent one-fourth of our life there, and the kids had spent most of theirs. The announcement of our departure was far more difficult than any other thing I had ever done in public speaking. It was almost as difficult as being in the hospital watching my dear friend and parishioner die. With that said, in 2021, at just the right time, God opened another door and bid us to step through.

Home can now be found in the Sandhills of Moore County, NC. I serve as the Senior Pastor of Pinehurst UMC (we prefer to say "one of the pastors" but a memoir demands exact titles, I suppose). Pinehurst UMC is, at the time of this writing (and has been for many years prior to my being there) one of the biggest, healthiest, and fastest growing churches in the United Methodist connection in North Carolina.

Pinehurst is known as the golfing capital of the United States. Each year, Moore County welcomes thousands upon thousands of visitors to play at one of forty golf courses within a twenty-mile radius of the Pinehurst Resort. Not only is Pinehurst a destination for tourists and visitors, but it is also a destination for retirees. That reality has long been the case. A newer reality that continues to push the growth of the area is the influx of military families moving into the county.

With Fort Bragg (formerly Fort Liberty, and also, weirdly, formerly Fort Bragg) a short drive away, families who have a higher housing stipend far prefer the Moore County lifestyle to the one around the post. What has resulted from this new populace, is a more diverse population in all the ways that you can contemplate diversity. It is a great place to be and to lead. I love the community I am a part of at the church and in the community at large, just as I loved Faison, and just as I loved the Pulaski of my early childhood. It is quite true, that there are days that I struggle to believe that my life is my life. It is that good in the here and now of our current homeplace.

With all of that said, ministry is still ministry, and since death still happens, ministry can be heart-wrenching, overwhelming, and traumatic. One weekday in the spring of 2024, Thomas, our Youth Leader, walked gently into my office. One of our youth group members that we had long been worried about had been found in his bedroom unresponsive. EMS was called, CPR was administered, his heart began to beat again, and he was placed in an ICU room at the local hospital, on life support.

The youth, a senior in high school, was a son of a mother who had recently been diagnosed with ALS. The progression of the disease within her had already become rapid. The young man's father is a United Methodist clergyperson; a good man with much to bear. The young man's brother was, and is, a standout human who does almost everything right.

All of us and others, at various times, gathered around the recently-turned 18-year-old for a few days; keeping watch, hoping and praying for a miracle. As I stood around and praying over his machine operated body, I could not help but think of so many friends long passed: "So this is what it looked like."

The wounds from the deaths many years ago had either mostly healed or scarred over. As I stood over this teenager, I could feel a new wound festering inside me and growing with every passing minute. After a few days the latest scan pictures of this young man's brain came back, no activity, no miracle. Opioids take life again. Cause of death: accidental Fentanyl overdose.

His parents, brother, two other folks (one also a pastor), Thomas and I, gathered around his body as we awaited the removal of the ventilator. His mother, who at this point, was barely able to speak due to her condition, said the best she could, "I wish I could sing. He loved it when I sang to him as a little boy." Within a couple of seconds, those of us able, join in the singing of *Amazing Grace*. A few minutes later, they unhooked his body from the life support machine. They pumped him full of the narcotic that put him there in the first place. His body showed what technically could be called signs of life, before one last gasping breath.

Prior to this moment, I had watched several people die in varied circumstances. I wasn't prepared mentally and emotionally on any of those occasions. I certainly was not prepared that day in May. There he laid, like so many of my friends and other young people. Gone too soon. A victim of something insidious and evil. Shattered hearts, all around the room. Soon, hearts broke within a youth group, a school, a church, homes, and so many other places and spaces.

Among the elderly and afflicted, death sometimes shows up as a welcomed guest. Never is this the case with young people. When death shows up for the young, what accompanies is in no way welcome. What accompanies is pain, and unrelenting and unfathomable sorrow.

Hurting as I was, I did not weep until the night following his funeral.

"God is with us" was my refrain that day in the sanctuary when we worshipped God and celebrated this young life. I reminded those gathered of what happened in Bethany when Jesus' friend died. I reminded them, and myself, of Mary and Martha and their broken hearts. When Martha and Mary saw Jesus they lamented, "Lord! If you would have been here." Jesus was moved. And there, finally *with* them, Jesus wept. What a strange thing for a God to do.

There in Bethany, Jesus, wiped a tear from his eye, looked at the place his beloved Lazarus' body lay, and he said, "Take away the stone." Then he called Lazarus by name. And out from the tomb came Lazarus. And Lazarus lived, *with* God.

Sometime later, his sister Mary, with tears filled in her eyes, looked at the place her beloved Jesus' body was laid and wondered, "How did the stone roll away?" There appears a man, ironically, she assumed he was the gardener, the one who tends things, the one who makes possible the growing of things, the one who pulls the weeds and reaps the harvest, the one who labors all the time out of love, the one who takes the manure that happens in life and utilizes it so that there may be beauty in the midst of life's messes, she rightly assumed he is the Gardener and then she says, "Where is my Lord? Tell me where you have taken him." The one who once said, "If you only would have been here," now says, "If you have carried his body away, tell me where you have taken him." And in an instant, God *with* us said her name, "Mary." She heard her name from his lips. Upon that hearing she was overwhelmed with joy. In that moment, all the if's of life lost their power.

Why? Well, because. Reminders matter. In the midst of life, we are in death. In the midst of death, we are in life.

After placing his remains in our memorial garden, as is my custom I stayed behind as the family went back inside to spend time with those gathered that day. I used my hands as I always do, and I covered him with the dust from which he and the rest of us came. I spoke a non-liturgical word over his remains and walked slowly to join the family, the colleagues, the bishop, friends, and acquaintances who were inside.

I went immediately to my office to catch my breath and hide. My spirit was broken. The last thing I wanted to do was to go out post-funeral and hear people tell me how great of a job I did preaching a funeral for an 18-year-old kid who reminded me so much of me. No matter how well you judge a funeral sermon to be, people will always tell you that you did a great job. Sometimes you just don't want to hear it.

After emerging from my hideout and mingling for as long as I could, I headed home. That night, with one heavy pour of bourbon after another, along with a heavy heart, I wept like I had not wept in several years. Deaths like that of my friend in Faison, and of this young man, caused a woundedness in me that my spirit was not equipped to handle. The cycle of unhealthy ways of trying to cope had accompanied me from Faison to Moore County. I guess the unhealthy coping methods followed from one county to the next because I came too. Heavy drinking was my misguided attempt to heal pains that I knew could not be healed in such a fashion; due to my lack of spiritual conditioning, I couldn't help it. Even with the fresh reminder that such substances rob life, I turned once again toward death in the midst of death.

As I drank and wailed the night of this young man's funeral, my two youngest kids, in that moment teenaged, came to console me, along with Amber. One of the kids asked, "What's wrong with dad?" Amber replied, "Sometimes your dad's job is really tough."

That week, that young man became a part of the company of hosts, in the presence of God. He also now resides in the core of my memory with all the others I have known who are gone too soon. Gone, but not forgotten.

Later the night of my drinking and weeping, I woke up from my sleep, screaming in terror. All I could see were his eyes. His big, beautiful eyes. Looking, dead, at me. Given the chance, I would have switched places with this young man. I didn't have the power or opportunity to do it though. But Christ did. And he did.

35

Elegy

From Exit 94B off Interstate 81, if you can find your way to Route 11, eventually you can turn left on Alum Spring Rd. Then, in less than a mile, you will have the opportunity to turn the same way onto Snider Lane. As far as I know, most days Michael can still be found in his childhood home on the lane. The last time I saw Michael is when I came to preach a few days at Jordan's Chapel in 2014.

Keith's family can still be found two doors down from Michael, in the home their son died in. On the opposite end of the lane, the blue house that Winky and his family lived in and kept chickens behind, has sat abandoned for years. They all now live in another part of the county on a stretch of land that encompasses a 500-acre farm I used to hunt, once tended by an Uncle, now tended by Big Wink. A former dairy farm, it's a beautiful piece of land with a mix of rolling pastureland and steep wooded ridges. There are ponds for the cattle scattered throughout the landscape. It's a great farm, and a good ways away from Snider Lane. I have been on the farm many times since the last time I saw Little Wink in person. It is going on two decades.

When you see Snider Lane to its completion, just past the old white church by the creek, turn left on Alum Spring Rd. and then the very first right will take you to where Adam's body lays. Looking straight out back behind his grave, and then also to the right, you can catch two of the best rolling hill views in all of Pulaski County. The day we buried him, Vince Gill's, *Go Rest High on That Mountain* played. His place of rest may not be a mountain, but it is close to some, and the views are just as good as any mountain view around.

Elegy

Stay on Alum Spring and you will see Adam's parents' place on top of the hill. Thankfully, they are still there. Turn right on Largen Hill and the Burton shack still stands. It has not been occupied in well over thirty years. A man did buy it decades ago for the sake of the piece of land beside the house. He built a garage there to store race cars.

The bus driver died not long ago, the shutters and roof are still green. There is no garden. The school bus that had been parked below the house has not been there in years. I'm not sure if her family still lives at the next house up, but I do know blessed Mary's innocent life was cut short due to health conditions that were complicated by her Down's Syndrome.

Get to the top of the hill and there sits my Aunt Alma and Uncle Neal's place, now occupied by some other family. They have chickens in the yard, and I love that. Priscilla and Manny are still across the road, Dina's car remained parked behind the house under a metal carport for many years, but no more.

The house with the rebuilt kitchen across from my grandparents is now owned by a sheriff's deputy. Maw-Maw and Paw-Paw and J.W.'s house is now unoccupied. First bought by a couple who could not keep up with the mortgage, the bank foreclosed, and empty it remains. Across from my dad's place, you will no longer find Duck there; he died in his thirties due to cancer. Following a family tenant or two, a good old boy named Johnny lives there now.

Betty and Elwood's house is now remodeled and occupied by people I do not know. Betty lived long enough to bury not only Duck, but all three of her children. The preacher Jimbo still lives on the next lot over from Betty and Elwood's old place. Jimbo's daughter now occupies his daddy's house with no live bait to be sold. The church beside the Largen double-wide has not had a service in more than fifteen years. Where there once was a basketball goal in the parking lot, there now remains only a stub of a pole.

My childhood home, a brown double-wide setup in 1985, is still there on a gorgeous two-acre lot. As surreal as it still seems, my father is no longer inside the house. Amber and I had tried to convince him since 2017 to move from the hill and in with us; at that point he had already been in failing health for a couple of years. Dad struggled with COPD since the late 2000's and congestive heart failure since 2017. We tried harder to convince him to make the move at certain times depending on the situation and season. We tried our hardest on June 30, 2025.

They Call Me Jabe

On that day, Amber and I made an unplanned 3-hour trip from our home in Moore County, NC to Pulaski, so that we could go see him in the hospital and tried to convince him to move in with us. Prior to that day, he had a few extraordinarily bad days. Over the phone, and with Johnny's urging as well, he finally agreed to go to the hospital on the morning of the 30th. By the time Amber and I got there, Isaiah now in tow, he had already left against doctor's orders. When we got on the hill, we found him in his chair, smoking a cigarette. We begged and bargained. I reminded him that 20 years ago in that same room, we had a seriously conversation that led to my life being changed thanks to his words. I was there trying to do the same for him. As the television continued to play, he rolled a half-lit cigarette back and forth in his little brown, glass ashtray with his head resting in his palm as he gazed off into nowhere in particular it seemed. He remained stern and steadfast, that he was not ready.

He was obviously the most ill that he had ever been. Two days later, early in the morning, he called me crying. We talked daily, always at night. I was almost always the one who did the calling. This morning call, initiated by him was heart-wrenching. An ominous feeling began to overtake me. It was apparent that dad was afraid and overwhelmed with what his life had become. My intuition, though unproven, tells me he learned something at the hospital that was too much for him to bear.

A couple of days after that heart-wrenching phone call with my weeping father, Ella convinced him by phone to move in our place. The date he agreed to move was on the 19th of July. We ordered everything we needed to get him set up in a room at our home. The stuff began arriving on Saturday. The two kids still at home were excited to help Amber set it all up.

That Sunday, July 6th, I did something I had never done before. After preaching in the first two services, I found myself sitting and waiting for the opportunity to preach in the third and final service. Something came over me. I was no longer satisfied with the sermon I had. When preaching time came, I abandoned my notes, walked into the pulpit, told those gathered that I felt the call to leave the day's sermon behind, and then I preached that life is hard and there is nothing wrong with admitting it, and lamenting it.

Sunday afternoon, just before 1:30, the phone rang. I knew it was the sheriff's office number showing up as the caller. A friend from high school and basketball was a deputy on the scene on Largen Hill Ct. He told me my father was found deceased in his bed. Sammy passed away at the age of seventy.

Elegy

The folks from the former Stevens Funeral Home showed up and carried the last Largen off the hill; never to return. After receiving the news, I ended the call. I turned the television off and sat in silence for over three hours.

Sammy Largen was a great man, father, and friend. He was a great ambassador for Largen Hill. Except for a four-year stretch, he lived his entire life there. We held his funeral in Jordan's Chapel, where I once again stood behind that church's pulpit. Their pulpit, where I first felt called into set-apart pastoral ministry. "Made for moments like this," I thought as I stood behind the pulpit that mournful Tuesday in July. I may have said half the things I wanted to say that day. Like I said, surreal.

We placed my father's remains beside his brother, at the feet of his mother, near his father. The four of them, together again.

After dad died, I was hit with a harsh realization, Largen's are a lot like my friends, there are not a lot left. A lot of my pondering time is spent wondering, "Where did they all go?" and "Why did they have to go?" Some questions do not have answers. Usually, if not always, the hard questions that ask something about God's action or lack of action in the world, fall into the category of the unanswerable. Not answerable from a human perspective anyway, and certainly no answers with any level of certainty. Over time, I have become more ok with that. All the Largen's and all my friends are still missed, nonetheless.

A few months before my dad died, I had another harsh realization that led to a commitment. A commitment to never drink alcohol again, in good times or in bad, in celebration or in grief. Although I never became an "around the clock" drinker, and kept it to mostly drinking in the dark of night, it was still unhealthy when I did partake. I discovered, admitted, and confessed that death had been dictating my health for far too long in my years of non-narcotic and narcotics use. Just as was the case in 2005, it was time for a change. I owed it to the father who saved me, who I in turn unsuccessfully tried to save. I owed it to myself. I owed it to my family. I owed it to all who I loved, and who loved me. I owed it to the God who not only called me but saved me by grace, successfully, time and time again.

If I was to preach that death had been swallowed up in victory, it was past time for me to swallow my pride and fear, and to trust the God who by grace had shown me time and time again that there was a better way that is full of life. I confessed that it is my truth that I cannot use substances, no matter how "legal," or how much or how little, no matter how successful I am, and still be able live into the fullness of life that God has gifted unto me. Nor can I lean more fully into the relationship that I have with God, trusting in his grace, if I am finding myself the least bit dependent upon mind-or mood-altering substances to try and fill the voids that only Gods-own-self can fill.

Addiction will not prevail. Woundedness caused by grief will not prevail. Death will not and does not prevail. There are better ways to cope, and I have known that all along. A move once again had to be made from knowledge to practice. Since that decision, wounds have healed. Depression has not been a factor in life, not to say that it won't at some point. There is no desire for any other way of living, nor for any feeling that is not naturally present within me.

With sufficient grace, vigilance, and help from others (including medical professionals), that is how it will be; never again, never a drop. Paradoxically, just for today.

36

Kairos

AFTER MY DAD'S FUNERAL, I got behind the wheel of his truck, a black 2014 *Honda Ridgeline* with the short bed, pulled it out of his little half-paved driveway in front of the double-wide and onto the hill. I headed off the hill, turned left, and then down Alum Spring Rd. until I got to the stop sign that forces a turn onto Route 11. I turned right and made my way through the Town of Pulaski, and eventually to a few different interstates, and across the state line into North Carolina.

About three hours after departure, far from any ridges, I pulled the *Ridgeline* into the driveway that has a black and white sign that says "128 Largen" to the right at the entrance. Nestled in the beautiful Sandhills of North Carolina, the driveway leads to a sturdy-built grey house with an outstanding water view from two-thirds of the structure. Sammy would have loved the view, but not as much as he loved the hill. Gratefully, Amber and I pay a mortgage on this grey house with the view. Who would have ever expected? I would not have.

After I put the black truck in park, I got out, walked up the steps and onto the porch and through the front door. Upon entering, as is the case nearly all the days, I was greeted by three dogs and two cats. After moving to Moore County, we grew to a three-dog home. Why not? What made the animal part of the family's greeting different on the day of my return is that it seemed as if they sensed that I was no longer the same person. They were right. Dealings with death cannot help but to change you. Gratefully, after the reintroduction to our four-legged babies, it was clear that they loved me still. As do so many others. I cannot believe how fortunate I am to be loved by so many, from so many different places. The stack of "Thinking of

You" type cards that were piled up on the island when I got home, proved that love is true.

As I entered our home that week after my dad's breath gave out, I found my family had made it so that our sunroom was furnished with my old bar, totally vacant, and a new bed and other furniture in it; already paid for and all set up for my dad.

Seeing the sunroom in that state made me weep again, this time, only a little. I wept, not for the room or its state, but for the absence of my father. My father who we remaining Largens tried to get in that sunroom turned bedroom before he died, but who never belonged there, "in Carolina" as he called it. He died on the hill where he always belonged; we should all be so fortunate. That hill in Pulaski County was his fate. The heartbreaking thing is not in where he died, but in that he died younger than he should have, like his father, not because of booze or dope, but because of cigarettes. "To each their own," I have heard it said.

When my people in Moore County, NC found out that my dad had just turned 70 when he died, most of them remarked, "Oh, he was young!" Most of them looked at me strange when I responded by telling them, "Not where we come from."

After wiping my cheeks dry and exiting the sunroom that steamy July day of the post-funeral return home, I went into the living room and turned on the television. I prayed a breath prayer. Amid the background noise of the Vizio, I pondered the opportune time before me to make the most of the gift of life still to be received.

I grabbed my MacBook.

I began to type.

As I typed, I reminded myself as I had been, that indeed, I am called pastor, preacher, reverend, doctor, coach, friend, son, husband, dad, pop, and a whole host of other things. But also, never to be forgotten lest I die too soon, "I am an addict; they call me Jabe."

I mustn't forget.

As we traverse this existence, full of fleeting moments that we call time, which is constantly bursting forth from the limitlessness of eternity, I believe what is memorable, matters most.

Therefore, I wrote the memorable down, before the final fleeting moment comes and goes, like a thief in the night.

KAIROS

Who am I? What kind of man am I? What evil have I not done? . . . But you, O Lord are good. You are merciful. You saw how deep I was sunk in death, and it was your power that drained the well of corruption in the depths of my heart."

—AUGUSTINE, *CONFESSIONS*

www.ingramcontent.com/pod-product-compliance
Lightning Source LLC
Chambersburg PA
CBHW062225080426
42734CB00010B/2036